# San Francisco Ghosts

Copyright © 2007

Mark Lyon

All rights reserved. No part of this book may be reproduced in any form, except for the inclusion of brief quotations in a review, without permission in writing from the author or publisher.

Library of Congress Control Number: 2007931545

ISBN 9780979532740

Second Edition

Windwhistle Press
12364 Summit Ridge Drive
Nevada City, California 95959
530-265-6877

# San Francisco Ghosts

Mark Lyon

Windwhistle Press

# Acknowledgments

It would be impossible for me even to attempt to list individually and to thank properly the scores of librarians, historians, writers and friends who so patiently, pleasantly and generously have given of their time and expertise throughout the course of my research and the writing of this book. Without their help it could never have been written.

I would be negligent, however, if I did not express a special debt of gratitude to the late Father John B. McGloin S.J. who first sent me out in search of San Francisco ghosts and suggested that I chronicle their stories, the late Helen Holdredge who not only answered many questions about Mary Ellen Pleasant's "House of Mystery" but also shared with me a long lost treasure trove of some of the city's best ghost stories and Gladys Hansen, Archivist of the City of San Francisco, Emeritus, who, as she has done for so many before me, gave so very much of her knowledge, invaluable insights, enthusiasm and greatly appreciated encouragement.

Finally, I must express my most profound thanks to Eleanor Yeatman and Richard Kleeberg for so kindly agreeing to proofread and critique my manuscript.

# Contents

| | |
|---|---|
| Preface | 11 |
| The House of the Howling Demons | 15 |
| The Ghost in the Window | 31 |
| Concepción and Nikolai | 38 |
| The Octagon House | 50 |
| The Tower Phantom | 54 |
| The Haunted Hill | 58 |
| The Sailors' Home | 65 |
| The Crystal Dress | 70 |
| The Kearney Street Poltergeist | 75 |
| The Fatal Prescription | 77 |

| | |
|---|---|
| Broderick | 81 |
| The Faithful Chorister | 89 |
| Duncan's Castle | 91 |
| Ghosts of the Golden Gate | 97 |
| The House of Mystery | 104 |
| The Ghostly Parishioner | 123 |
| The Atherton Mansion | 128 |
| Joaquin Murrieta | 134 |
| Waiting in the Rain | 141 |
| The Ghosts of Golden Gate Park | 143 |
| The Sixteenth Street Terror | 147 |
| The Curse of Sutro Heights | 151 |
| Presidio Ghosts | 156 |
| Chinatown Haunts | 162 |
| Hoaxes, Humbugs and Other Spurious Spooks | 170 |
| The Haunted City | 176 |
| Together | 192 |

# Preface

When thin, gray wisps of fog drift in from the bay and the mournful cry of a foghorn calls out from over the waves, San Francisco becomes the perfect setting for a ghost story and, for well over one hundred and fifty years, San Franciscans have recounted stories of the many ghosts said to haunt their city's fabled hills.

But, you may ask, "Do ghosts really exist?" That is a question to which I can answer with an unequivocal "Yes." There is far too much evidence to believe otherwise. Certainly, many "hauntings" may, upon investigation, be explained away as the misinterpretation of natural phenomena or as the result of an hallucination or conscious fraud and, as we shall see, San Francisco has certainly had its share of these. But it is impossible to dismiss the hundreds of carefully authenticated cases in which credible and unrelated witness have described seeing exactly the same apparition or have experienced the same "ghostly" phenomenon in the same place without being aware of the other witness' experience. These cases lead to the inescapable conclusion that ghosts do, indeed, exist. As The Bard put it, "There are more things in heaven and earth than are dreamt of" in our earthbound philosophies.

When we ask the question, "Just what is a ghost?" however, the subject becomes much more complicated. Many theories have been advanced over the years and a great deal of controversy has ensued.

Some believe a ghost to be the spirit or soul of one who has died and has, for some reason, remained bound here on earth. Perhaps, they suggest, the spirit suffers from some deep psychological problem which prevents it from realizing it is dead and, thus, from passing on to "the other side."

Or, perhaps, as in the chapter "Waiting in the Rain," it is a ghost with a purpose, desperately trying over and over again to accomplish some important last act or to resolve important unfinished business. Often, as in the case of the "Faithful Chorister," the ghost only appears once, at the time of death or shortly thereafter, never to be seen again.

Another theory suggests that ghosts are not living, thinking entities at all but merely a kind of psychic impression created by an unusually emotional event which has imprinted itself into the surroundings in which it had originally occurred and, like an eternal motion picture, continually replays itself over and over again. Such may well be the case with the ghost of Concepción de Argüello.

Then there are poltergeists — noisy, mischievous and sometimes dangerous ghosts which move physical objects — leaving no doubt as to their presence. Parapsychologists have long suggested that such phenomena are not "ghostly" at all but are, instead, the result of an unconscious, uncontrollable telekinetic ability on the part of someone on the scene. But while this seems the most likely explanation in many cases, it fails to explain such hauntings as "The House of the Howling Demons" in which both physical phenomena and apparitions were observed.

I personally believe there are a number of very different types of phenomena which, for want of a better term, we collectively call "ghosts" and feel it would be a mistake to assume any one theory could be used to explain them all.

Are the stories in this volume true? Now, that is a much more difficult question to answer with any certainty and, perhaps, it is not my place to make such judgments. The intent of this volume is neither to explain nor to prove the existence of these or any ghosts. My purpose is merely to relate the experiences of those who claimed to have encountered the otherwise unexplainable and to recount the fascinating stories behind the phantoms said to haunt a city which has, for so long, enchanted so many with its color, history and unique charm. The stories collected here have been gathered from personal interviews, historical narratives and newspaper accounts and, in each case, the tale was originally presented as being entirely true.

In telling the stories behind the ghosts and haunted houses of San Francisco, however, I have had to trust in the reliability of the original sources upon which earlier historians have based their accounts. As history is always subject to revision upon the discovery of new facts, this can often be more risky than confronting the most frightening of ghosts at the stroke of midnight.

This may be particularly true in recounting the life of Mary Ellen Pleasant, a legendary life in which fact and fantasy have become so entangled over the decades that it may well be impossible to ever know for certain what is true and what is not.

While in such cases I have attempted to carefully sift out the truth, I must concede that a few of the historical "facts" are open to question. In telling these stories I have, on occasion, taken the artistic liberty of making a few assumptions and filling in small details where the historical record is incomplete. But in no case has any important fact been knowingly changed or distorted.

Finally, it must be assumed that there is still a wealth of wonderful San Francisco ghost stories I have yet to hear. If you know of a story which I have missed, have had an encounter of your own with the paranormal or can shed more light on one or more of the stories included herein, I would be most delighted to hear from you!

Mark Lyon

# The House of the Howling Demons

Colonel John Pool Manrow seemed strangely quiet and preoccupied that September day in 1856 as he met with his friends at the headquarters of Second Committee of Vigilance. Sullen and remote, he seemed to have drifted far off into a world of his own. Suddenly, he looked up and quietly asked, "Do you think the dead can come back to haunt the living?"

"What?" someone asked in surprise.

"Ghosts? Do you believe in ghosts?" the colonel asked.

"Surely, you are joking," a skeptic responded.

But they needed only look at their friend to know that he was deadly serious. The words came slowly and deliberately as he continued. "For over three months now, strange things have been happening in my home. Things for which I can find no other explanation."

His friends sat dumbfounded as Manrow recounted how his Russian Hill home had inexplicably come under siege by seemingly supernatural forces. Without warning, inanimate objects had taken on lives of their own, flying about the room. Horrific phantoms materialized out of the evening air and terrifying shrieks emanated from the house at all hours of the night.

If anyone else had made such a statement, he would not have been taken seriously. But John Pool Manrow was a man who had earned his friends' respect. Formerly an engineer and now a highly successful businessman and Judge-Advocate of the Second Committee of Vigilance, the forty-year-old Englishman was admired for both his mental agility and personal courage; his only eccentricity being a passion for riding to the hounds each morning with his beautiful wife, in the manner of a country squire, in pursuit of the foxes, coyotes and wildcats which shared the surrounding countryside. But even this was done with such style and panache — he with the hunting horn to his lips and she in an exquisite riding habit — that their morning ritual served only to add an even more dashing and colorful aspect to his personality.

Still his story was beyond belief and two of his friends, a lawyer, William H. Rhodes, and mining engineer, Alamarin B. Paul, accepted Manrow's offer to visit his home and observe the phenomena first-hand. Thus on Friday evening, September 19, 1856, the two men set out from their home on the southern slope of Russian Hill to begin what was to be the most baffling and incredible adventure of their entire lives.

It was a clear, cool evening and an almost full moon was beginning to rise as they reached the summit of Russian Hill, stopping for a moment to catch their breath and admire the object of their quest. Perched upon the western slope, on the northeast corner of Chestnut and Larkin, and commanding a breathtaking view of the bay, Manrow's fanciful Swiss chalet appeared to glow phosphorescently in the moonlight. Constructed of iron and shipped in sections around Cape Horn, the house was a fantasy of high-pitched gables, dormer windows and leaded glass adorned with fantastic carvings, spires and ornamental ironwork which hung like lace from its numerous eaves. Crowning the peak of each roof were rows of turnip shaped finials. An English garden of hollyhocks and roses completed the fairy tale atmosphere.

By eight o'clock they had reached the front door where they were greeted by the colonel and ushered into the library. "May I introduce you to my wife, Eliza," he began, presenting a demure young woman with light blue eyes and long blond hair and then continued by introducing her sister, Mrs. Benedict, and the latter's fourteen-year-old daughter, Mary.

As they were ushered into the library where they sat down around the large cherry wood table, Paul asked the ladies if they were frightened by the strange occurrences.

"Oh, no. Not now," Mrs. Manrow replied. "It was terrible at first. But now we're all rather used to it. If they were really malevolent and tried to hurt us, that would be one thing. But, actually, they're quite childish and do the silliest things. Yesterday I found all the salt had been emptied into the sugar bowl and the sugar was in the salt box.

"And today I bought a wonderful hat downtown. When I got home, I laid it upon the piano. I looked away for only an instant and then turned back to glance at it again. Every feather had been plucked from the bonnet!"

Mary's bright eyes flashed with unabashed excitement and Paul wondered if, somehow, she might be responsible for the ghostly pranks. There was only one way to be certain. While the others lightly placed their hands upon the table in the hope of encouraging communication from the spirit world, Paul took up a position outside the circle where he could observe everything and detect any possible trickery.

They waited a few moments in silence. Then, slowly, the table began to move. A knock was heard somewhere from within the room — then another. Then the heavy table began to rise from the floor as an almost continuous succession of raps and thumps were heard emanating from the table and from almost every other part of the room as well. All five participants clearly had their palms resting flat upon the table but, incredibly, as Paul stared in amazement, the immense table rose a foot and a half from the floor and floated in midair as lightly and gently as a fallen leaf dancing upon an autumn breeze.

They next darkened the room by removing a lamp. But, as the moon had by now filled the room with a silvery glow, every person and object could still be scrutinize with perfect accuracy. Rhodes asked that each member of the circle hold his neighbor's hand tightly to preclude against deception while Paul continued his watch from a distant corner.

Suddenly, almost every object in the room seemed to come alive. Books flew from their shelves, sofa and chair cushions were hurled about in all directions and the doorbell began to ring violently. At the same time, everyone came under personal attack. Some were slapped or struck by phantom hands while others were pulled by their hair, kicked by spectral feet or poked and pinched by invisible fingers. All the while they endeavored to hold hands even more tightly, the circle remaining unbroken. Meanwhile, Paul flailed about in an attempt to block the blows he was receiving and, perhaps, catch his assailant. To his horror, each of his frantic swings met nothing but empty air.

By the time the barrage had ended, Paul had become convinced that the phenomena were, indeed, genuine and he sat down at the table with the others, joining hands with two of the ladies. As if in answer to his joining the circle, a book immediately flew across the room, striking one of the ladies on the chest. Paul picked it up and placed it upon the table. The book flew open before him. Mystified, Paul closed the book.

But, again, the book flew open. Paul turned down a corner of the page to mark the place and, when a light was produced, found on the indicated page the question, "Cannot ye discern the signs of the times?" — the only scriptural quotation in the entire volume. Perhaps, they reasoned, this was a sign that the spirits were ready to communicate. So by means of a rapped alphabet code, they began to communicate with a spirit who claimed to be the ghost of James King of William, the crusading newspaper editor whose assassination had given rise to the Second Committee of Vigilance.

"Have you any message for us?" Manrow asked.

"None," the spirit answered.

"Was it you who has appeared before my family for several evenings?" Manrow continued.

"It was," the spirit responded.

"Will you appear tonight?"

"I will."

"What sign will you give?"

"I will ring the doorbell."

Breathlessly they waited for several minutes in silent anticipation. But, as pulses quickened, an eerie quiet hung over the house. Then the doorbell began to ring frantically and the front door shook as if something possessed of enormous strength were attempting to enter by force. The house dog began to bay and growl ferociously at the unknown intruder. Colonel Manrow ran to the door but, upon opening it, found no one there. Courageously, he walked the perimeter of the property and searched the grounds but all to no avail. No mortal hand had pulled the bell rope.

No sooner had he returned than the doorbell again began to ring. But again the martyred newspaperman failed to materialize. They began to wonder if it might be some other spirit masquerading as King. To test this theory, they questioned the spirit further. Although the first two or three questions were answered correctly, when they asked, "How long have you been dead?" an incorrect answer was given.

Again they asked the spirit to identify itself and, this time, the name "Capitana" was rapped out. Mrs. Benedict gasped. Capitana was the name of an elderly Kanaka woman she had known in the Hawaiian Islands who had died a few years before.

"Will you not appear to us?" the colonel asked.

"I will," the spirit tapped back, promising to announce her appearance by ringing the doorbell.

Almost immediately, the doorbell rang and a large bush growing near the east window began to shake violently. As they looked toward the window, they clearly beheld a human figure silently glide to within two feet of the window, not ten feet from where they sat unable to move. But before they could focus clearly upon the details of its form, the specter vanished.

As Rhodes sprang to the window, another phantom rose up before them. Unlike its predecessor, however, this was the most frightening form of which the human mind could possibly conceive.

It appeared, as Rhodes would later record, "in the moonlight, silent, still and sublime in its horrible deformity. If all the fiends in Hell had combined their features into one masterpiece of ugliness and revolting countenance, they could not have produced a face so full of horrors. It was blacker than the blackest midnight and over its head and body it had spread a mantle of the most stainless white, looking like a robe of new fallen snow covering the blackened remains of a conflagration. It seemed as though personified sin had snatched the garment of a seraph and spread it over its own thunder scarred and Hell scorched form."

Its face was turned toward them in profile and wore "an expression of cruelty and revenge darkened by the frown of everlasting despair."

As if in a trance, the others drew toward the window and, petrified with horror, gazed transfixed upon the terrible wraith. Suddenly Rhodes felt physically sick and filled with a desperate need to immediately flee the house and escape into the fresh air. He rushed for the door, quickly followed by all but Paul, who fearlessly maintained his position by the window. As they fled the library, tables, chairs, rugs, fire pokers and cushions suddenly flew up into the air as if attempting to block their passage and sailed about the room in all directions. As Rhodes ran out of the room, a cushion from the parlor struck him on the head and one of the ladies was almost blinded with dust as a sadly neglected chair covering flew up toward her.

Just as they reached the door, the front gate tore itself loose from its hinges, flew up a flight of ten steps and wedged itself tightly against the front door so as to keep the door from swinging open, thus, preventing their escape.

Panicked, they ran back, hoping to escape by the kitchen door. By this time, however, the phantom had vanished. In its last moments, Paul had watched as the dreadful apparition, then not more than eight feet away, lightly lifted its robe from the ground and gently glided off a few yards toward the barn before it evaporated into the evening air.

Mrs. Manrow's mother and two of Mrs. Benedict's younger children, aroused by all the noise, also clearly saw the apparition from an upstairs window and watched with an hypnotic-like fascination until, at last, it disappeared from view.

Dazed and terrified, the group reassembled together in the library where they stood utterly speechless, staring at each other in stunned amazement. As for Rhodes, he had experienced quite enough for one evening and adamantly refused to have anything to do with forming another circle. But after having a chance to collect himself, he finally relented upon the condition that they should attempt to call up only friendly spirits.

No sooner did they sit down and make their wishes known than Rhodes felt a cool delicate hand running its fingers through his hair, gently caressing his cheeks and forehead. At the same moment, each of the others felt similar soothing hands softly stroking their brows, cheeks and hair, though each member of the circle was still holding tightly to his neighbor's hand.

Then Paul announced that he could see the phantom hands and hardly had the words escaped his mouth before Rhodes also beheld them floating about before him. At first they were faint, almost invisible. But gradually, over the course of five or six minutes, they grew more and more palpable until, at last, he saw them as clearly as if they were made of flesh and blood.

There seemed to be at least a dozen of these hands and they seemed to be as gentle and loving as the previous spirits had been horrifying, as if they were striving to make amends for the pain and terror caused by their predecessors.

The colonel, who had been suffering all evening from an excruciating toothache, asked if they might be able to ease his pain. At once, several hands began to tenderly massage his jaw and continued to do so until the pain had completely disappeared. These new spirits identified themselves as their celestial guardians and further soothed and enchanted the circle with kind and uplifting personal messages. The hour had, by now, however, grown late and the group reluctantly adjourned for the night.

Baffled and amazed, Rhodes and Paul met secretly a number of times over the next two days to compare notes and convince themselves as to the reality of all they had encountered. Their accounts matched perfectly down to the smallest detail, as well as matching Manrow's memory of the evening. Finally satisfied beyond all doubt that neither had they been duped nor had they been hallucinating, the following Saturday night the two men found themselves battling an unusually ferocious, cold and wet westerly wind as they again climbed Russian Hill in the hope of repeating the previous night's adventures.

Thick banks of fog formed ominously before them as if the spirits had conspired to make their journey even longer and more perilous. As Judge-Advocate of the Vigilantes, Manrow had passed sentence of death upon four men. Could the ghosts of those whom they had hung, they wondered, have come back to haunt him?

At last they saw the lights of the unique iron house and soon they were warming themselves before a cheery fire as the ladies came downstairs to join them.

They had seated themselves around the library table and were about to begin when the Manrow's bloodhound began to bay and growl. Everyone looked to the window in expectation but nothing materialized. Still the bloodhound bayed. Bravely, the colonel opened the front door and walked out into the thick fog. A few moments later he returned, not pursued by a menacing ghost, but with a mutual friend who had been wandering out in the mist for over an hour. He had attempted to find a shortcut over the hills but had succeeded only in becoming lost amidst the fog and the darkness. He had been attacked by at least half-a-dozen dogs and had lost his hat in the process. He now stood before his friends bareheaded, cold, tired and dripping with condensation from the mist but eager to join their circle.

Again they sat down around the table and joined hands. Soon the table began to rise from the floor and, again, ghostly knocks began to emanate from all parts of the room. But were these spirits the guardian angels they so hoped to meet again or were they the mischievous and terrifying goblins they had come to dread? After about half an hour, this question was rudely answered when both Rhodes and Paul were violently struck in the face, on the head and upon other parts of their bodies.

Paul next felt a pair of spectral hands riffle through his breast pocket where he kept the large key to his safe. Within moments his companions saw the key slowly rise out of his pocket and then fling itself onto the table. No sooner was this accomplished than the ghostly pickpocket set to work on a watch which Paul wore on a ribbon about his neck. Breathlessly they watched as the timepiece floated over his head, suspended itself for a moment in the air and then carefully floated down to the table. Wishing to test the spirits again, the ribbon was placed around Mrs. Manrow's neck. Again the watch rose into the air, hung tantalizingly for a moment in midair and then playfully dropped down into her bodice. At the same time other ghostly hands continued to search through Paul's clothing until they found a small pincushion in his vest pocket which they quickly appropriated and threw down onto the table.

All the while each member of the circle was continuously assaulted, poked or stroked by invisible hands. At one point Rhodes was struck so hard in the right eye that tears began to form and he felt compelled to complain. Immediately at least six phantom hands reached for his handkerchief, gently used it to wipe away the tears and then began to massage his face until the pain was gone. Once they had succeeded in soothing both his pain and his temper, however, the spirits quickly resumed their impish behavior and insolently dashed the handkerchief across the table and into one of the ladies' bosom.

The colonel had previously mentioned that he had often heard ghostly voices, closely approximating the human voice, but softer and less distinct, along with whistling throughout the house and grounds and Rhodes challenged the spirits to demonstrate these talents. He let out a loud shrill whistle. At once another whistle echoed back. Again and again he whistled and, each time, the ghost responded with an identical whistle. Finally he sent forth the most difficult, complicated whistle he could possibly devise and again the obliging whistler reproduced it perfectly note for note. Someone asked if more than one whistler could perform at the same time. Without a moment's hesitation, six or seven spirits improvised a symphony of whistling. They asked the spirits to move from room to room, performing first in the parlor, next in the hall, then the piazza and even out-of-doors. In each case, their requests were granted.

"Can you speak to us?" they asked the spirits. Suddenly the air was filled with the murmur of ghostly voices, low indistinct whispers which seemed to be whistled forth rather than articulated. Paul's name was clearly called out and several sentences were spoken to him. A girl's name was whispered three or four times into Rhodes' ear but he could not quite catch the rest of their message.

Next the doorbell began to ring wildly. Paul sprang to his feet pointing to the window through which a small figure could clearly be seen in the moonlight. The spirit, a young girl, perhaps ten or eleven years of age, cautiously approached the window. She darted back and forth several times and then vanished.

Without warning another spirit appeared at the window within six feet of them. This was too much for Mrs. Manrow who let out a terrified scream. No one, however, was more terrified than the ghost who, upon hearing the scream, quickly retreated into the kitchen, passing through a solid wall along the way! Gathering up its courage, a few moments later, the phantom emerged part-way from behind the wall, standing half in and half out, as if wondering whether he should attempt another foray. This ghost was tall and thin and, although clearly human in form, unlike the others, seemed composed more of shadow than of substance. Uncertain of what to do, the timid spirit again retreated through the wall and then reappeared and retreated several times until finally, in apparent frustration, it floated away.

It was now past midnight and the group decided to attempt one last experiment. Throughout the night Paul had been a favorite target of the spirits, having been thrown several times from his chair. As a final test, the spirits were challenged to pick Paul up into the air and throw him down onto the table. Before he could even prepare himself, Paul felt something grab him by the collar while something else lifted him headlong into the air and tossed him onto the table. Although he landed with a tremendous crash, Paul found to his surprise that he was completely unharmed by the fall. The flight, however, ended any desire on Paul's part for further experimentation that night and the group agreed to meet again the following Friday evening.

The next five days seemed to drag by for Rhodes and Paul as they impatiently waited for the appointed evening to arrive. Thus, they were disappointed when, upon their arrival, they learned that Mrs. Benedict and her daughter would not be present that evening. And to make matters worse, Mrs. Manrow had been ill all week and was suffering from a cold. Still, she would join the circle and, undaunted, the remaining four again joined hands around the table.

Several minutes passed without the slightest indication of any spiritual activity and Rhodes was about to suggest a postponement when, at last, the table slowly began to move and a loud succession of raps and creaks and bangs echoed throughout the room.

The spirits became so excited and vociferous that several minutes passed before intelligible communication could be established. These, it seemed, were the guardian spirits of the first evening. Their purpose, they explained, was to protect the group from the "dark and evil spirits" they had encountered earlier.

The group next tested the spirits' telepathic abilities. One member of the circle would silently think of a number and ask the spirits to respond by tapping out the number chosen. Almost without exception, the spirits answered correctly.

Then, for some time, all became deadly still. The four waited, tightly holding hands. A rustling was heard from under the bookcase ten feet away. The noise became louder and louder until, with a violent start, several large maps which had been rolled up and hidden there flew out into the center of the room. One of two large globes, mounted upon short legs, rolled out from under a recess beneath the bookcase and headed toward the circle. It passed under the table, finally toppling over as it emerged from the other side. At almost the same moment, the other globe began rolling toward the opposite window. Just before reaching the window, it increased its speed and smashed into one the of the lower panes with such force that it shattered the glass.

The doorbell began to ring and hearts pounded as each member of the group turned their eyes to the window. Again the bush at the window began to shake wildly as the small young girl they had seen a few nights before appeared and drew close to the window, only to fade away a moment later. Next a strange light appeared at the window. It was like a large globe lantern but it cast no shadow and danced about in the night air like a will-o'-the-wisp. Again it approached the window, only to recede back again, changing shape from circular to oblong to irregular. Back and forth it darted from one side to the other, continuously changing shape all the while. Finally, it settled close to the ground and assumed the unmistakable shape of a newly dug grave. It lay there, almost six feet long, an ominous heaped-up mound, glowing with a ghastly phosphorescent glare — a pale glare which shown brighter than the full moon. Then it stretched out into a thin narrow line, slowly melting away into nothingness.

A voice rang out in the darkness. "Colonel, help me! Help me!" it cried. A moment later they observed Colonel Manrow's manservant running madly toward the house screaming, "They're after me! They're after me!" Manrow rushed to the front door allowing the terrified man into the house. As he stood trembling in his torn nightshirt, he tried to explain. "I was sleeping, just mindin' my own business, when they come after me. I tried to fight 'em off but there was too many of 'em. They knocked me out of bed and started tearin' at my clothes."

The poor man was given a place of refuge in the piazza while the remaining four returned back to the library. Hardly had they again seated themselves at the table, however, when a terrible thud was heard in the entryway and the servant again cried out in pain. Back to the entryway they ran, only to find the hapless man sprawled out on the floor, having been struck on the cheek with a blow so savage as to produce serious swelling.

Fearing that the spirits were now becoming far too dangerous, the four reluctantly called an end to the seance.

In the months which followed, the spirits continued their

mischievous behavior, flinging flower pots against the wall, spewing water about, extinguishing the lights and terrorizing the entire neighborhood with their screaming and howling throughout the night. The denouement came, however, the day a playful spirit hurled a hatchet at the colonel's head, missing him by only a fraction of an inch. Not long thereafter, the Manrows retreated to the safety of a downtown hotel and had the house sealed with new locks.

Their departure did nothing, however, to help their Russian Hill neighbors. For although the house was bolted shut with no mortal residents inside, the night air continued to be pierced by horrifying screams which echoed still throughout the house and garden. One by one, the terrified neighbors also began to move away. Before moving away to a more pastoral life in Grass Valley, one neighbor, Lola Montez, gave Manrow's deserted home the name by which it would forever after be known: "The House of the Howling Demons."

Perhaps it did have something to do with the Vigilantes' resurgent reign of terror. Perhaps, through the violence they committed in the name of justice, they had unknowingly opened an unseen door into a world of evil. For not long after the Committee of Vigilance disbanded, the howling seemed to lessen with each successive night until, finally one night, it stopped entirely. After a while, Manrow felt it was safe to return and, in the weeks which followed, found that the spirits had left as mysteriously as they had arrived.

Although the ghosts had departed, the house's ominous reputation remained. Years went by and, as the Manrows passed into the twilight of their lives, they allowed the home which had once been a center of San Francisco society to fall into disrepair. The white paint which once glistened in the sunlight faded and peeled. Rust stains trickled like dark tears down its iron walls and, one by one, its once proud ornaments fell from the roof. One day Eliza died and the colonel followed not long thereafter.

The sad, empty house was sold for taxes and the new owner, John Klumpke, attracted rumors like a magnet. He was a bit of an eccentric. He looked at the weather-beaten old house, peacefully rusting away, and saw no reason to change things. He liked it that way. And soon passers-by would point to the house and whisper about the strange old man in the Prince Albert coat and high silk hat who was said to sit up all night in an upper room, counting his gold. Treasure, they said with a knowing look, was hidden in the loft of the old stable.

And stranger still, the ghost of John Pool Manrow was said to have returned to the house, tramping through the rooms at night with mud-stained boots and jangling spurs. Each morning, they said, you could hear the blast of his horn as he rode off to the hunt. Manrow, it seems, had passed from history into legend and from the haunted to the haunter.

When John Klumpke died in his nineties, the windows were boarded up and the wonderful iron house was left abandoned by all but memories until, in 1918, it was torn down and a tall modern building rose up in its place.

So very much has changed since that September evening when William Rhodes and Alamarin Paul first climbed Russian Hill in search of the unknown. Yet if you stand there today and, for just a moment, you allow yourself to become engulfed by the wind which so often whips up around one at that particular spot, it is not hard to imagine that, perhaps, a few spirits may still remain, hiding in the shadows – waiting to, one day, return.

# The Ghost in the Window

It had been just an ordinary Monday early in December of 1871 the when children knocked at the door of the house at 2119 Mason Street. When the tenant, Mrs. Jorgensen, answered the door, they asked about the strange man in the window.

"What man?" she asked.

"The man in the upstairs window," they repeated.

Mrs. Jorgensen knew there was no one else in the house but, half out of curiosity, she followed the children out into the street. They pointed to an upstairs window where, indeed, she saw the ghostly image of a man wistfully looking down onto the street below. He was quite handsome. He had sad, pensive eyes, sported a mustache and goatee and wore a shirt with a short straight collar and a dark cravat. His hair was parted in the middle into short, graceful waves, a lock of which fell gently over his forehead. Amazingly, however, the gentleman appeared not to be standing behind the window but seemed to be, somehow, actually formed within the glass itself!

Mrs. Jorgensen rushed upstairs. She looked to the window but, from the inside, saw nothing unusual. When she went back down to the street, however, there was the strange man still sadly looking down upon her from the window.

Not knowing what to make of the mystery and, perhaps, a little frightened, she called out several neighbors who were just as amazed as she. They, too, ran upstairs and searched the small room for anything which could be causing the ghostly image but no solution was to be found.

Word spread like wildfire and soon the street was filled with the curious who congregated below Mrs. Jorgensen's window. Rumors spread with equal speed. "An invalid had once lived there," one said, "and he used to sit by that very window, looking just like that!"

"No," someone else would respond, "didn't you hear? It's the ghost of Mr. Jorgensen. He died just about a year ago in Sweden."

"I heard from someone who should know," a clearly knowledgeable spectator volunteered, "that a woman once lived there whose brother cheated her out of a fortune. That's his spirit, trapped there in the window! They say you can never rest with ill-gotten gains."

Reporters eagerly jotted down every word while spiritualists joined hands around their tables in search of an explanation from the other world.

The size of the crowd increased daily and, by Friday, several thousand came to stare on a single day.

In the days which followed the crowd would begin to gather before dawn and would remain there until nightfall caused the image to temporarily fade from view. Mason Street, between Lombard and Chestnut, became so crowded that it was nearly impassable. Streetcars in the vicinity enjoyed record business from dawn till dusk.

By Saturday, Mrs. Jorgensen had endured quite enough. She was tired of reporters banging on her door at all hours. She was tired of explaining to the curious, "No, that is not my late husband. And, no, I don't know who it is!" She was sick of the noise, her nerves were frayed and she longed to regain her privacy.

Then she hit upon the ideal solution. She would sell the ghost. After all, if the streetcar companies could profit, why shouldn't she? She would sell the uninvited guest, she announced, for ten thousand dollars.

Rumor again held sway. "Barnum has telegraphed to purchase it," a street sage confirmed.

"No, the North Beach Railroad Company has bought the house in order to draw passengers," someone else corrected.

At half-past eleven in the morning, the widow's landlord fought his way through the Mason Street crowd and offered his tenant twenty-five hundred dollars for the mysterious window. Then, perhaps realizing that he was actually buying his own property, he lowered his price to a more reasonable twenty-five dollars. Mrs. Jorgensen was not amused and refused to give up the ghost.

Not long afterwards, R. B. Woodward arrived at her door desiring to purchase the ghost for his combination amusement park, menagerie and museum of curiosities in the Mission district. Behind closed doors, they negotiated. Soon a stunned crowd gasped as the lower sash containing the ghostly image was removed from its frame and the upper sash dropped down in its place.

The haunted sash was quickly wrapped up in a sheet and spirited off to the law office of Judge E. D. Sawyer where Woodward carefully examined his prize and, over the protests of a representative of Mrs. Jorgensen's landlord, for the princely sum of two hundred and fifty dollars, he became the proud owner of a bonafide ghost.

Meanwhile, back on Mason Street, hundreds of spectators continued to stand out in the cold wind, looking up toward the open window. Perhaps the ghost might materialize again on the upper sash, they reasoned.

For almost two hours they waited, searching every window for an ectoplasmic sign, until someone announced that the ghost had reappeared around the corner. Some held their ground fearing it might be a trick by which they might lose their places in front of the original window. But others quickly ran around the corner where, only a few doors down, at the 708 Lombard Street residence of J. J. Hucks, a second apparition was, indeed, materializing in a window.

Perhaps, some theorized, the ghost resented being sent away to be exhibited with the wild animals at Woodward's Gardens and had left Mrs. Jorgensen's window to claim a new place of honor in his old neighborhood. But no! As the curious strained to get a better look, they saw that it was an entirely new ghost, more vivid and colorful than the last. And, whereas the first ghost had been young and handsome, this new phantom was quite elderly and somewhat grotesque in appearance, his nose resembling a bottle-gourd.

Soon hundreds had gathered to admire the new ghost and, when Mr. Hucks returned home, the surprised axle grease baron was besieged with requests to enter his home and determine whether, like the first ghost, this new one could be seen only from the outside. Realizing that resistance would only prove futile, he invited a few reporters into the house. They inspected the window and tried their best to rub the image away. But despite their most vigorous efforts, the ghost refused to budge. In fact, he looked a lot better for having been given a thorough cleaning!

Although the crowd was delighted, Mr. Hucks was not. He

had his fill of ghosts for the day and, upon seeing a reporter from the *San Francisco Chronicle* making a sketch of the ghost, he almost became almost violent, shouting that he wanted "no such damned thing as that put in the *Chronicle* about his house." The reporter, however, would not be moved and continued sketching until the exasperated owner pulled down the blinds and the ghost disappeared from view.

No sooner had this ghost vanished, however, than a third one appeared in the window of a house at 2109 Mason Street, just a few doors up from Mrs. Jorgensen's. It was in the shape of a large butterfly with spotted wings which tapered down gracefully toward the ends. But once it had succeeded in attracting a crowd, this new phantasm, just as mysteriously, faded away.

Then a man, so excited that he had only bothered to don one boot, came running down Mason Street proclaiming that still another ghost had been seen on the southeast corner of Mason and Green. But his description would be forever lost to history for the last reporters to remain on Mason Street had already seen their quota of ghosts for the day. As one reporter later explained, "It was getting rather monotonous, this ghost business. So we determined not to interview this fourth abomination."

Before the day was out, R. B. Woodward visited Mr. Hucks, who was only too pleased to also sell his ghost for two hundred and fifty dollars (that being the going rate for ghosts.) By Sunday, the original window had been installed in the second story of Woodward's museum where the ghost could happily gaze down upon the grounds. Early that morning a notice had been affixed to Mrs. Jorgensen's door explaining that the ghost had been moved to Woodward's Gardens and advising those interested to "Go there and see it." And thousands more, each paying twenty-five cents apiece, did, indeed, go to see it, each speculating as to the cause of the mystery.

Even His Imperial Majesty, Norton I, the eccentric and self-proclaimed Emperor of the United States and Defender of Mexico, visited Woodward's Gardens and issued the following edict:

IMPERIAL CHAMBERS,

December 11

Be it declared — That I, in the interest of sound faith and the progress of scientific research have caused a strict and careful investigation to be made concerning the sensational rumors afloat in this city, and I find that there is no reason to believe in any supernatural agencies at work among us.

The figure on the window is the correct likeness of some man, evidently of foreign birth. While looking out of the window while the glass was under some peculiar circumstances, and at the time when his stomach was disordered either by indigestion or intoxication, the acidity of his breath has caused his image on the glass to have been permanently impressed.

However, for a final judgment in this matter, I defer my subjects to the advice of my wise men and caution them against listening to either seditious statements or scoffers.

NORTON I

But even a decree signed by the imperial hand could not dissuade the multitude of true believers who again braved the cold winds and assembled Sunday morning below Mrs. Jorgensen's window. After all, the faithful reasoned, if it really was a ghost, what was to prevent it from appearing again in the remaining sash? As each streetcar arrived, the crowds became even larger.

Hour upon hour they stood there, freezing from the cold. But then, just as the clock struck half-past twelve, someone announced a miracle. A small, faint spot of light appeared upon the center of the glass. As it became larger, someone proclaimed it to be the ghost's neck. Then, within moments, a man's beard came into view. Soon the entire profile began to materialize. Or so, at least, the chosen said, for the newspaper reporter present was unable to see anything at all.

As each newcomer arrived upon the scene, he would ask, "What can you see?"

"Don't you see it?" they would answer. "The ghost is coming back."

Confused, one reporter went back to his office where he wrote:

> Quoth the Judge to the Captain
>   "Pray what do you see?
> I'm just a little near-sighted
>   Just show it to me."
>
> "I see," said the Captain -
>   "I see a great host;
> They've nothing to do
>   But to watch for a ghost.
>
> "If they don't see a ghost,
>   They'll catch a bad cold
> But they never will own
>   How badly they're sold."

# Concepción and Nikolai

There still exists within the Presidio of San Francisco a small fragment of the old Spanish Trail which once linked its *Comandancia* to Mission Dolores. It is known today as Lover's Lane. And if you retreat from the noise and the rush of the city into the gentle calm of its hidden embrace, if you allow yourself to meld into its pastoral enchantment, you may see her — walking slowly — just ahead of you. And if you pause for a moment to gaze back from the old brick footbridge, here again, you might see her. And if you linger at twilight near the former Officers Club, which now stands where she once lived and knew her sweetest moments of happiness, here too you might see her — standing quietly, watching and waiting, gazing serenely toward the bay — the perfect embodiment of faithfulness and a love which will endure forever.

It all began so very long ago on a cold April morning in 1806 just as the sun began to rise over the Contra Costa hills. Baron Nikolai Petrovich Rezanov, Chamberlain of Russia, Imperial Inspector of the Northeastern Colonies and Plenipotentiary of the Russian American Company, gave the order to weigh anchor and the brig, *Juno*, stole silently from out of the fog in which it had lain hidden throughout the night and ran straight for the Golden Gate under full sail.

So very much depended upon this moment. When the baron had arrived seven months earlier at the Russian colony of Sitka with an imperial commission to investigate the condition of the Alaskan settlements and make whatever improvements he could, a nightmare had awaited him. The threat of starvation hung like an ever darkening cloud over the colony of two hundred desperate men. One supply ship was already known to have been lost and another had failed to arrive. If but one pound of bread per day were to be issued to each man, their stores would be depleted in only a few weeks. Their supply of dried fish and seal-meat was equally low and efforts to catch fish had proven fruitless. Eagles, crows, manta rays — anything that could be eaten — was eaten. And winter was moving in fast upon them.

As a freezing rain fell, seemingly without end, the appearance of scurvy added the specter of an agonizing death to miseries of almost every kind. Rezanov wrote, "We live in Sitka only upon the hope of leaving it."

But, just as all seemed lost, the American ship, *Juno*, had sailed into Sitka's harbor. Rezanov immediately purchased the ship and its entire cargo and embarked upon a daring plan. He would fit out the ship with an assortment of trade goods and set sail for the Spanish settlement in California in the hope of trading his cargo for grain. He was well aware that Spanish law forbade all trade with foreigners and that the authorities might even refuse entry into their ports but he no longer had a choice. With many of his crew already suffering from scurvy, he set sail for California.

The months of depravation, however, had taken their toll. Soon half his crew was so weak that they were unable to carry out their duties and the number of sick increased daily until they were all stricken with scurvy. After an agonizing voyage lasting almost a month, his crew, with pallid corpse-like faces, at last beheld the Golden Gate.

But guarding the bay with unknown armaments was the fortress Castillo de San Joaquin. Could they sail past the citadel under the cover of darkness, Rezanov wondered? He had to try. But soon the fog became so dense that they could no longer see the coastline. They vainly attempted to run soundings but, finally, Rezanov decided to take no further chances and cast anchor just outside the entrance to the bay.

The next morning, at first light, Rezanov decided upon a desperate run straight through the Gate and past the Spanish guns. It would be sheer folly to ask permission, for if it were denied, they would all surely perish at sea. By comparison, the risk of a few cannon balls seemed no risk at all.

As the *Juno* drew near the fortress, the Spanish soldiers began waving their fuses as if threatening to fire. But the cannon remained silent.

"What ship are you?" shouted a Spanish soldier through a speaking trumpet.

"Russian!" Rezanov answered.

"Drop your anchor! Drop your anchor!"

"Si Senor! Si Senor!" the Russians shouted back, pretending confusion until they were well past cannon range. The *Juno* then cast anchor in the safety of the harbor, so close to shore that it was possible to set out mooring lines.

Almost immediately seventeen horsemen galloped from the fortress to the shore where they demanded the surrender of the ship. The Russians lowered a boat and Rezanov sent a midshipman, Lieutenant Davydov, and the ship's physician and naturalist, Dr. von Langsdorf, as emissaries to meet the horsemen. Once on shore they were received by a Franciscan monk who, as none of the Russians spoke Spanish, conversed with the doctor in Latin. The monk introduced a young man wearing a striped sarape over his uniform as Don Luis de Argüello, the son of the commandante and acting commandante during his father's absence. Lieutenant Davydov cautiously began by stating that their ship was part of a Russian voyage of discovery and that, although they had intended to present themselves first to the Spanish governor at Monterey, contrary winds and a scarcity of provisions had forced them to put into San Francisco in the hope of obtaining permission to purchase supplies and make necessary repairs to the ship.

Don Luis had heard of Rezanov and had received orders from the King of Spain stating that, should the Russian ships come to San Francisco, they should be treated with the greatest of hospitality and furnished with any supplies they might desire. But Don Luis was wary. Why, he asked, did Baron Rezanov come in the *Juno* when, according to the dispatch from Madrid, the Russian expedition consisted of two ships, the *Neva* and the *Nedezhda*, commanded by an entirely different set of officers than those of the *Juno*?

The lieutenant said a silent prayer and replied that the original ships had been sent back to Russia and Rezanov had been ordered by the Czar to continue aboard the *Juno*.

Don Luis thought for a moment and then smiled warmly. "I would be honored," he said, "If Baron Rezanov and your fellow officers would dine with my family tonight."

When the Russians arrived at the simple adobe home of the Argüellos, they found awaiting them a warmth and generosity beyond all imagining. For the first time in months, Rezanov felt the spirit of hope arise within his soul. But even more miraculously, for the first time in over three years, he felt stirring within him emotions he had thought long since dead. For over three years he had grieved over the death of his wife.

And for over three years he had immersed himself entirely in his work, convinced he would never love another. But now, as he was introduced, one by one, to the Argüello family, his eyes fell briefly upon Don Luis' sixteen-year-old sister, Concepción, called Concha by her family.

Standing against the rough whitewashed walls of the *Comandancia*, she seemed a delicate flower, as perfect as the pink Castilian rose held within the gentle waves of her soft lustrous hair. When she smiled, he felt, somehow, warmer, as if caressed by a summer breeze. Her long dark lashes hid, for the moment, the sparkle of her eyes and betrayed the simple innocence of a girl unlike any he had ever known before. Graceful in movement, almost perfect in face and form and, yet, simple and entirely artless in her manner, she lit in his heart a flame which he had long believed to have been forever extinguished. For the moment it was only a small flame, as that of a single candle in the vast darkness of eternity. But it was a flame which might be kindled and fanned until, at last, it might burn as brightly as the most brilliant star in the heavens.

Perhaps, as some men seem to know their destinies from their earliest days, he knew from that very first instant that their lives would be forevermore entwined. But, for the moment, the lives of his men depended upon him and Rezanov had to content himself with only an occasional fleeting glance at the beautiful young girl as he conferred with Don Luis and the Franciscan fathers following dinner.

Upon returning to their ship, the Russians were to glimpse the full measure of Spanish hospitality. Awaiting them was enough food to supply their company for days: pounds of onions, garlic, lettuce, cabbages and other assorted vegetables along with four fat oxen and two sheep. But this was to be only the beginning.

The next day they visited Mission Dolores where they were treated to a feast of wondrous variety: vegetable and bean soup, roasted fowl, leg of mutton, salad, an assortment of vegetables prepared in a variety of ways, cheese, pastry, preserved fruits, tea, chocolate and wine.

Rezanov hastened to reciprocate the following day by presenting their hosts with carefully chosen gifts. Don Luis was given a prize English fowling piece. The Franciscans each received a length of fine English fabric as well as cloth of woven gold for the decoration of their church. For Don Luis' mother and sisters there were shawls almost four yards in length, delicate muslins, printed cottons and striped ribbons. There was no one who did not receive something especially desired and the goodwill between the Spanish and their guests grew even stronger.

Rezanov dispatched a courier to the Spanish governor in Monterey asking if he might be allowed to visit him there in the hope of gaining permission to trade his cargo for the grain and other foodstuffs so vital to his starving colony. The governor, however, courteously replied that he would not think of imposing such a journey upon his guest. He would, instead, leave for San Francisco on the following day and sent orders ahead instructing that the Russians be assisted in all of their needs.

While awaiting the arrival of the governor, the visitors spent most of their time in the company of the Argüellos. Hardly an afternoon went by without the pleasure of music and dance. To the accompaniment of violin and guitar played by the soldiers of the garrison, the Argüellos taught their guests the *barrego* and other Spanish dances while the Russians returned the compliment by teaching their hosts English country dances. And, as they danced, the baron found himself being drawn closer and closer to the beautiful young girl who had so enchanted him only a few nights before. Her dark eyes flashed as she threw back her head dramatically in the seductive *barrego*, her lithe young body becoming one with the music. Rezanov felt the flame of passion grow within his heart.

She offered to teach him Spanish and each day, as they walked slowly along the old Spanish trail or sat in the cool of the evening looking out over the bay, his feelings for her grew. There was always something new, something even more wondrous about her yet to be discovered.

He loved her voice — soft, gentle, sweet, and warm. In her voice was balm with which all the sorrows of the world might be healed and all transgressions forgiven.

And in her eyes he saw beauty, compassion for those in need and the paradox of strength made even stronger through vulnerability.

Gradually, emotions he thought he would never again feel began to swell within him. He longed to embrace her, to kiss her, to gently glide his fingers over every detail of her face. The fragrance of her hair and the scent of her skin whispered through his days and haunted his nights.

And from almost the first moment she saw him, Concha knew the handsome Russian would be the only man she would ever love. She was considered to be the most beautiful woman in all of California and many were the suitors who flocked to her father's door. But none had been able to win her heart. Now, however, unreservedly, she wished to give not only her heart but her destiny as well to this stranger from a faraway land.

Finally, one day the Russians heard nine cannon blasts heralding the arrival of Governor Don José de Arrillaga and Commandante Don José de Argüello and, at last, Rezanov was able to begin negotiating for the grain he so desperately needed.

Trade between the two colonies, he suggested, would be of benefit to both Spain and Russia. Not only would they be able to satisfy the needs of both the Alaskan and the Californian settlements but they would also establish lasting bonds of friendship between their two countries. "The colonies of both," he continued, "would flourish and, as our coasts form a tie between us, our mutual protection would be assured. We would be equally protected by each power. Nobody would dare to settle in the unoccupied territory between us."

Rezanov's arguments were persuasive and the venerable old man liked his young visitor but he shook his head slowly. "There is so much more to consider," he said sadly. "I have received word that our two countries may, as we speak, be at war with one another."

"That may be true," Rezanov replied, "but we are in such a remote corner of the world that we may hear of war when peace has already been declared."

"My friend," said the governor with a gentle smile, "if only it were that simple."

When they met again the next day the governor was troubled. "I wish, with all my heart, that I could give you all you have requested," he began. "But I do not know how to do so. You cannot imagine how strictly the regulations against trading are enforced. The most I can do is to allow you to buy grain from the missionaries. But the viceroy in Mexico will never allow you to sell your cargo here."

But both men knew that there would be little room in the *Juno* to store grain unless Rezanov also sold his trade goods. Another solution had to be found.

"What if I were to pay for the grain in cash?" Rezanov suggested. "The receipts could then be sent to the viceroy who would have no reason to object. And should the holy fathers then desire to use their money to buy from me goods of which they are greatly in need, it would be of no concern to either you or the viceroy."

"No, that would be the same as trading," the governor replied. "After living sixty years without reproach, I cannot take that upon my conscience."

"But it would be done not out of avarice but rather out of a desire to help your people," Rezanov implored. "You are in a much better position to judge the needs of your people than are those in Madrid. How can there be any sin in it when the priests will all fall down onto their knees in prayer for you?"

The baron paused momentarily, searching for just the right words. "I have no desire to cause you trouble. I merely ask you to give me hope that some way will be found."

"My friend" the governor answered, "with God's help, you shall have it."

As Rezanov anxiously awaited an answer from the governor, he spent as much time as possible with Concha. With each day he began to treasure more and more the hours spent with her and, with each day, he came to feel more and more that the hours away from her were empty, hours wasted. Finally, he realized that she was the cause of a happiness he had thought he would never again know and he knew that, without her, he would forevermore feel incomplete.

Finally one evening, just as the full moon began to rise, he took her trembling hands into his and asked her to become his wife. She smiled and, with a kiss, melted into his arms.

Her parents were horrified. True, they thought the world of the dashing Russian and had come to feel as if he were a member of their own family. But marriage — no, that was impossible. The baron was a heretic, a member of the Eastern Orthodox Church! It was unthinkable that a daughter of the

Roman Church should marry outside of her faith. In desperation they turned to the Franciscans who dragged poor Concha into church, made her take confession and pleaded with her to renounce her intended. "You must choose," they warned her, "between this man and Christ!"

But Concha knew her own heart and refused to give in and the priests, finally worn down by her resolve, reluctantly concluded that such a decision could only be made from the throne of Rome.

This was agreeable to Rezanov. Not only would he go to Rome to gain the necessary dispensation but, immediately following his return to St. Petersburg, he would go to the king in Madrid and attempt to smooth out any misunderstandings between Russia and Spain. Such a journey would be hard and it would be at least two years before he could return to claim his bride but, looking deep into Concha's eyes, he knew that he had no other choice.

Concha's parents, who could deny their daughter nothing, then gave their blessings to the union on the condition that the betrothal be kept a secret pending the pope's decision. And, not long afterwards, the governor agreed to a complicated plan by which Rezanov would receive his grain without violating the specific letter of the Spanish law.

Then the day came when the lovers had to part. They embraced one last time and, with a touch that was a kiss, he gently caressed her hand.

"Two years," he whispered.

"Two years," she echoed as her fingers slowly slid from his.

As they sailed past the Castillo de San Joaquin where the Argüellos and other friends had gathered to wave goodbye with their hats and handkerchiefs, the Russians fired a seven-gun salute. The Spanish replied with nine. Concha stood straight and proud as the *Juno* sailed past the Golden Gate. But as the ship started to fade into the distance until, finally, she could see only the glint of the setting sun as it struck the copper hull of the disappearing ship, she found she could hold back the tears no longer and, silently, she sank to her knees.

The days seemed to pass so very slowly for the young woman but, gradually, days turned into weeks, weeks into months and months into years until, at last, two years had passed. Each day, sometimes for hours at a time, she stood looking out over the harbor, searching the horizon and praying that this day would be the day she would see the white sails of a ship bringing her love back home to her. Each evening she imagined his arms about her and shared the secrets of her heart with him as if he were actually there. But two years turned into three and three into four and still no word came as to her lover's fate.

Numerous suitors begged for her hand in marriage only to be politely turned away; for she would remain forever faithful to the only man she would ever love. Ten years would pass before she heard of her lover's fate and it would be another fifteen years before she learned the painful details.

It had been September by the time Nikolai had reached the eastern coast of Russia and, although he should have waited at least until spring, in his desire to reach St. Petersburg as quickly as possible, he had attempted to cross Siberia in the dead of winter. The privations of the previous year had taken a severe toll upon his health but still he slowly plodded thousands of miles on horseback through freezing rain and blinding snow until, at last, he was struck down with a raging fever and had to be carried into a Yakut hut. Rising from his bed before having a chance to fully recover, he continued on for twelve torturous days until, overcome by exhaustion, he could hold the reins no longer and fell from his horse into the ice and snow. He lay in bed for some time racked with fever but, again, he resumed his journey too soon, only to collapse one last time in the village of Krasnoyarsk, where he was laid to rest beneath an altar-shaped stone. It was said that, as he died, with his last breath, he called out the name of Concepción de Argüello.

Heartbroken, his beloved assumed the gray habit of a *beata* and dedicated her life to acts of charity and service to others, caring for the sick as well as teaching both Spanish and Indian children. In 1851 she was ordained as California's first nun and, when, four years later, a Dominican convent was founded in Benicia, she was chosen to become the convent's first mother superior.

Concepción de Argüello died at the convent in 1857 at the age of sixty-seven and, ever since, it has been said that her spirit haunts the Presidio — the site of her happiest hours. She stands looking out toward the bay, searching the horizon, patiently waiting for the return of the man she will love through the end of time.

# The Octagon House

Tucked neatly away amidst the bustling shops and restaurants of Union Street, at the corner of Union and Gough, there stands a small but precious jewel box of a house. Painted a soothing Wedgewood blue and accented with clean white trim, the Octagon House can cause even the most harried passer-by to stop for a moment, smile, and reflect upon a time when life moved at a more leisurely pace and was, perhaps, a bit more manageable.

Built in 1861 by William C. McElroy, a miller, and his wife, Harriet, on a Gough Street lot just opposite its present location, the house represented the most modern innovation in architectural design and health conscious living. Promoted by phrenologist, lecturer and publisher Orson S. Fowler in his book, *A Home for All*, the octagon-shaped house was thought by many to be the most cost efficient and healthful plan yet devised for residential architecture. For exactly the same cost required to build a conventional rectangular building, an octagonal house provided twenty percent more interior space. Moreover, large windows on each wall literally flooded the house with light throughout the day while a cupola with eight more windows provided a skylight illuminating a stairwell at the center of the house. The octagonal plan also allowed for more efficient heating of the home while ventilation necessary for cooling the home in summer and eliminating offensive odors was accomplished by simply opening one of the windows in the cupola. During the 1850's and 1860's, Professor Fowler's design became all the rage and at least five octagon houses were built in San Francisco. Unfortunately, only two have survived.

Until his death in 1871, William McElroy often employed one feature of the unique house in a manner even Orson Fowler could not have anticipated. Sitting up in the cupola for hours on end, McElroy had an unobstructed view of San Francisco Bay and would keep a sharp eye out for any ships in distress. Whenever he spotted one which appeared about to go under, he would race down to the harbor, jump into a waiting boat, row out to the sinking craft and, exercising a lawful right to salvage, take away anything he could find of value.

His widow continued to live in the house for another twenty years before renting it out to a local poet who, for three years, made the house a gathering place for poets and artists. This, no doubt, would have infuriated William who, back in 1861, had written a letter addressed "To Future Ages" lamenting the election of Abraham Lincoln and the fact that "our glorious Union is about to be dissolved." He had hidden the letter, along with newspaper clippings from 1860 and 1861 and a tintype of his family and an artist nephew, in a cylindrical tin box under the staircase leading up to the cupola. In his letter he clearly stated his unalterable belief that his nephew had not chosen a respectable profession.

Over the years, time, vandals and earthquake damage were all to take their toll on the house until, in 1952, it was sold for one dollar to the National Society of the Colonial Dames of America who moved the building across the street to its present location on land donated by two of their members. There the house was extensively and lovingly restored by the Society both for use as their meeting hall and as an exquisite museum of colonial art and furnishings.

As one enters the house, past the massive mahogany and bird's-eye maple grandfather clock and into a world of calm, graceful charm, the visitor cannot help but feel that here time, somehow, stands still. An oil portrait of James Madison's sister, Frances, presides over an elegantly appointed first floor featuring original Hepplewhite, Duncan Phyfe and Chippendale furnishings, fine china and silver, a Trumble portrait of George Washington and even a gilt Louis XVI chair used by the general, himself, in his Philadelphia White House.

Upstairs the enchantment continues in the form of a cozy bedroom with an inviting "press bed" which, in colonial times was pulled up into its canopy during the day. There is also a rich walnut Queen Anne chest-on-chest with a cleverly concealed secret drawer. Other rooms provide a comfortable library and an impressive display of rare documents containing the signatures of all but two of the signers of the Declaration of Independence.

Rising high above the second floor foyer is a gently turned spiral staircase reaching up into the cupola and it is up there that a mystery dwells. Long before the house was picked up and carted across the street, the Octagon House was thought to be haunted. On the night of each November 24th, it was said, ghostly footsteps could be heard climbing the stairs toward the cupola. When the phantom reached the twentieth step, it would stop for a moment and let out a horrifying, piercing scream. A soft thumping sound could then be heard, like that of a lifeless body falling slowly down the staircase. Then the house would be engulfed in a terrible silence.

In the course of restoring the house, the original central staircase had to be demolished to the level of the second floor and replaced with a new staircase climbing up the west side of the house. Only the staircase running from the second floor to the cupola was left in its original position. One might assume that this modification along with the moving of the entire house across the street would have discouraged even the most persistent ghost, but that, apparently, has not been the case.

In 1964 the California president of the Society surprised members of the city's Education, Parks and Recreation Committee by stating that the Octagon House was still haunted. "When we are meeting," she calmly related, "it is quite usual to hear footsteps on the stairs up to the widow's walk. But no one is ever there."

# The Tower Phantom

It was artist Bill Morehouse's first night in residence in the Spanish colonial style tower of the San Francisco Art Institute. In 1948, Morehouse, later to become the Chairman of the Art Department at Sonoma State University, was a student at the Art Institute and lived in the tower while serving as a night watchman and helping with the construction of a tower apartment for the janitor. He was camping out on the third level of the cheerless grey cement tower in a large room furnished only with a water tank and his bedroll and was about to retire around midnight when he heard the doors on the levels below him open and close. He then heard the sound of footsteps ascending the stairs. He knew he had locked the lower door but didn't think to investigate as he assumed it was only the janitor.

The sound of footsteps, however, kept advancing closer and closer until, at last, they stopped for a moment directly in front of his door. He saw the door knob turn. The door flew open and then, just as mysteriously, closed, followed by the sound of footsteps crossing the room in front of him. The unseen visitor seemed to turn around and then head back toward the door.

Again the knob turned and the door opened. Almost disbelieving what he had just seen and heard, Morehouse looked through the open doorway into the total darkness of the stairwell. No one was there. Then the door, once again, closed seemingly of its own accord. Morehouse found it difficult to sleep that night.

Bill Morehouse was to live in the tower from time to time over the next few years and was, along with several others who spent time in the tower, to often encounter the mysterious footsteps which were always heard ascending the stairs but never seemed to descend back down. They were described as being heavy and measured which made Morehouse feel the spirit to be that of a man. "I became used to it," he would later state, "sensing it was a benevolent kind of spirit."

He also recalled how one evening he and a few friends decided to have a party in the tower. They were laughing and talking when they heard footsteps climbing the stairs. He and his friends became absolutely still and waited until the footsteps were just outside the door. At that moment one of them threw open the door and yelled, "Surprise!" No one was there. Yet the phantom steps continued on their way to the top of the tower.

Stories of the Art Institute's ghost have persisted ever since the school opened its doors on Russian Hill in 1926 and its activities have not been limited to the tower.

Wally Hedrick, a former faculty member of many years, told of how, while once walking through the Institute's lower hall at around two or three in the morning, when no one else was in the building, the lights, controlled by switches at each end of the windowless hall, suddenly went out trapping him in darkness just as he reached the middle of the hall. Then, just as suddenly, he heard the sound of an assortment of machinery, including a table saw and lathe, starting up. He could see a faint light coming out from behind the door of the school's workshop. Cautiously he opened the door and, to his amazement, found every machine in the room to be running although no one else was there. Puzzled, he threw the room's main power switch and prepared to leave. As soon as he turned the corner on his way out, the machinery again started up on its own. It was sometime later that he first heard stories of the Institute's ghost who was promptly blamed for the unexplainable phenomena which continued to occur from time to time in the workshop.

The ghost seemed to have a special love for turning the lights on and off as Hayward King, later to become director of the Richmond Art Center, was to learn during the time he was the evening registrar at the school. Each evening at ten he would walk through the school turning out all the lights before locking the doors. Often, however, just before leaving, he would look back one last time to discover one or two lights glowing from within. One evening as he and Wally Hedrick were about to leave, all of the lights suddenly turned on simultaneously although such an occurrence should have been impossible, as there was, in those days, no master switch and each light would have had to have been turned on individually.

On other occasions, while walking through the darkened lower hallway, King sometimes felt "a draft of air and a strong sense of another presence." And, more recently, a student working in the Institute at around two in the morning suddenly heard footsteps behind him. He turned around to look, only to find that he was completely alone.

Although Bill Morehouse felt that the spirit was benevolent and that of a man, others who have experienced it disagree. A student studying in the library late one night with his wife recalled how they both heard the sound of what seemed to be chairs being smashed into pieces just behind them. No normal explanation could be found. "It's a mindless entity," the student stated, "a sense of energy vibrating, a damp feeling that goes through you." For a while things got so bad that the librarians refused to work after dark.

Although the ghost seems anxious to make its presence known, there has only been one report of it actually being seen. On that occasion, the figure of a young woman was observed standing on the observation platform at the top of the tower, picturesquely framed within its tall, arched, open windows.

Attempts have been made to discover the identity of the tower phantom. When, in October of 1976, a séance was held in the tower, it is said that a glass of water shattered although no one was touching it. And it was said the flame from a candle jumped five inches in the air. Still, the restless spirit remains as much a mystery today as when it first appeared well over eighty years ago.

# The Haunted Hill

Of San Francisco's forty-three hills, Russian Hill, named for a colony of Russian mariners who, in the days before the Gold Rush, called the hill home is, by far, the most haunted.

During the 1930's, local residents often reported seeing a spectral Russian seaman standing amidst the long grass and yellow mustard flowers on a rocky outcropping of the hill, gazing steadily toward the bay through a brass spyglass while bearded companions repaired heavy ropes and spat out what were presumed to be salty Russian oaths. Houses, now long gone, which had been built atop the forgotten Russian graveyard in the area of Jones and Vallejo Streets were said to be occasionally shaken by phantoms who periodically arose from their graves to make forays through the houses and out into the night.

Not far away, at 900 Green Street, there once stood a grand English manor house built by a shipping tycoon named Hanford for the woman he would soon marry. No bride, however, was destined to turn its stately rooms into a comfortable home or to fill the master bedroom with the warmth of her love. Some say Hanford's bride died before they could occupy the house; others suggest he was jilted. Whatever the truth may have been, the mansion was not to be occupied for years and it became known as a house in which strange, inexplicable things occurred.

Glowing eyes were said to peer out from within the darkness of vast halls made even more foreboding by unusually high beamed ceilings. Furniture allegedly moved about in the dead of night guided by unseen hands while the house echoed with fiendish laughter.

One night a high school student bravely ventured into the house only to flee in terror upon hearing a terrible crashing sound emanating from the floor above him and turning around to see a skeleton grinning back at him in a mirror. The next day a caretaker found that the tables and chairs in the music room had mysteriously been overturned.

Another ghost, dressed in rags and believed to be the spirit of a vagrant who had hanged himself in the basement, was often seen gracefully leaping over the home's formidable retaining wall.

In 1917 the house was rented by Sadakichi Hartman, one of the most flamboyant and eccentric personalities to ever grace a city well known for its tolerance of eccentricity. Half German and half Japanese, Hartman was an artist and always dressed the part. Appearing in public attired in an opera cape and black fedora, his long, thin, black moustache and sparse beard made him appear even more exotic. He was a painter, a playwright, an actor, a dancer, a poet and an art critic: a man of many parts. None of them, however, was modest. "I am a genius," he would proudly declare. "At nineteen I had read all the literature in the world!"

The flamboyant genius decided the Hanford House would provide the perfect setting for a fashionable salon, a gathering place for the city's artistic and intellectual elite. It would be, in his words, the "lair of the intelligentsia" and soon the howls of ghosts were replaced, or perhaps drowned out, by the strains of exotic oriental music which drifted out from within the house into the evening air.

Appropriately enough, Hartman decided to stage a production of Ibsen's *Ghosts* at the house, casting himself as the mentally deteriorating Oswald. Everything was going splendidly until the end of the second act when they came to the scene in which the orphanage catches on fire. At the very moment when, in the play, the conflagration is seen through Oswald's window, a real fire was seen burning a short distance away in Sadakichi Hartman's garden house. Although Hartman ran out into the street in a panic and claimed he had no idea how the fire had started, those who knew him felt certain he had thought a little fire would achieve just the right theatrical touch. He simply had not foreseen that the fire might grow far beyond the dramatic effect he had envisioned. Fortunately, the fire was extinguished before any serious damage was done and the play was resumed as if nothing had happened. Anxious that such a spectacle not be repeated, the police arrested Hartman, releasing him only after he promised not to stage any subsequent theatrical productions at his home.

In the years which followed, the mansion would be converted into a club and a tea room and be used for formal dances but it would forever be known as haunted.

Another Russian Hill house with a ghostly reputation was referred to by local residents as the "Half House." The "Half House" got its name as the result of an especially venomous divorce. The couple could agree only on splitting everything exactly in half. This included the house which was carefully sawn into two equal halves. One half remained where it had been built on Russian Hill while the other was shipped off to the

Mission District. Spirits which had previously lived in the house and were thought to be angered by the change were said to express their displeasure by pitching the beds about at night and scrawling enigmatic messages upon the walls.

Another historic house with a ghostly past is the charming Italian villa at 1032 Broadway which nestles half hidden by trees on a sunny part of the hill. Built in 1853 by Joseph H. Atkinson, a wealthy brick contractor who was later to be involved in the erection of an early building on Alcatraz, the home is thought by some to be the oldest house still standing in San Francisco. It was rescued from the fire of 1906 when the owners and a few of their neighbors defied evacuation orders and saved their houses by nailing cleats to the dangerously steep roofs and valiantly fought the flames with brooms, wet towels, sand and buckets of water drawn from nearby cisterns.

Over the years such literary giants as Robert Louis Stevenson, Bret Harte and Mark Twain, as well as numerous writers of lesser fame, visited the house with such regularity they were almost considered to be permanent residents.

Two part-time writers who actually did share the Atkinson's home on a regular basis were William H. Rhodes and Alamarin B. Paul who, after investigating the haunting of John Pool Manrow's home on the other side of the hill, became fascinated by the supernatural. Spurred on by both their close proximity to the old Russian graves and the ghostly phenomena experienced by the Manrows, they held numerous seances within the Atkinson House. After the lights were lowered and the house sank into darkness, rapping sounds could be heard issuing from deep within the rich redwood paneling, elaborately carved beams and furnishings. It is said the home still echoes with ghostly rapping.

Not far from the Atkinson House, one of the city's five

octagon houses was said to be haunted for a time by the spirit of an elderly spinster who was rumored to have hidden all her money in the attic. Every seventh night her ghost was purportedly seen knocking on a trapdoor in the ceiling. Eager treasure hunters were unable to find any of her supposed fortune but it was discovered that she had left behind some long overdue debts. Once the debts were paid, her spirit vanished, never to be seen again.

Quite a different kind of ghost story unfolded during the period following the Gold Rush in a house, long since gone, in a Spanish settlement which then flourished on Russian Hill. A heavy layer of dust and a garden choked with long Australian vines suggested that the large, elegantly furnished home had not been occupied for some time when Mary Addis, a widow with three young children, moved into the house and set up business as a washerwoman. The inexplicably low rent and strange "earthy smell" about the house added an air of apprehension to what otherwise would have seemed the answer to her prayers. In her bedroom stood a stately walnut bed along with a wardrobe and chests of drawers filled to capacity with beautiful Spanish clothing.

Despite the splendid furnishings and a breathtaking view of the bay, however, there was something depressing about the house, an unshakable feeling of dread. When she asked neighbors and those who had lived there before her about the home, she was told only that it was a "very bad house."

Not long afterward, her children began to speak of "The Lady," a proud, slender woman with shining black hair who wore a Spanish dress and who often mysteriously appeared in the house and garden. The woman, who never spoke a word, was no one they had ever seen in the neighborhood.

It would not be long before Mrs. Addis also saw "The Lady." One evening, upon returning home from shopping, she saw the woman standing in her doorway. Frightened, she dropped a parcel she had been carrying. She looked down for only a moment to pick up her package. When she looked back up again, "The Lady" had vanished. On another evening she again observed the same woman standing in the garden.

Then, a few nights later, she heard a plaintive moan. As her two youngest children had just recently recovered from a fever, she ran to their room in alarm. The children, however, were sleeping soundly. She heard the moan again. Only this time it sounded as if it had come from her own bedroom. When she opened the door she saw a young woman in a Spanish dress desperately attempting to rise from the large bed. Her face was wrenched in pain and terror. Standing over her was a man who threw her back down onto the bed and began to savagely beat her.

Mrs. Addis attempted to run to the woman's defense but, as she took her first steps into the room, everything suddenly went black and she fell to the floor. She had no idea how long she had lain there unconscious but, when she awoke, the woman was gone. She watched as the man pulled up a section of the matting covering the floor to reveal a large hole which had been previously dug in the earth. By the bed was a large narrow box which he then dropped down into the hole. Again everything turned to darkness and, when she next awoke, she found herself in bed, suffering from a fever.

As soon as she was well enough, Mrs. Addis sent for Isaiah W. Lees, Police Captain of Detectives. "The Lady," Lees was to discover, was not a ghost at all but the sister of a woman named Carmen who had lived in the house prior to Mrs. Addis and had, some time back, disappeared without a trace. "The

Lady" admitted to having often visited the house in the hope of finding some clue as to Carmen's fate.

Lees had three officers tear up the matting on the bedroom floor as well as the boards beneath and there they found a long box matching exactly the box Mrs. Addis had, in her vision, seen buried. Upon opening the box they found the body of a young woman wearing a Spanish dress. Her face had been obliterated with slaked lime. Examination by the coroner revealed she had been beaten and buried alive.

# The Sailors' Home

Until it was torn down in the mid-1920's, a bleak four-story building with a flat roof brooded down upon its Rincon Hill neighbors. Originally built in 1853 as a hospital but abandoned in 1868 after having suffered earthquake damage, the building reopened in 1876, under the auspices of the Ladies' Friend Society, as The Sailors' Home, a sanctuary for the sailor on leave and a warm and congenial last berth for ancient mariners.

But more than just the living resided within its stark walls. Mothers warned their children, "Don't play near that old building!" And late at night, and as the wind howled and the rain beat hard against the casement windows, men with sun-parched faces and gnarled hands, men grown old before their time, gathered around the iron stove in the reading room and spoke in hushed tones of the Home's secrets.

Now one of those who liked to talk of the Sailors' Home's unregistered guests was One-Eyed Welchy. Oh, he could talk for hours on end about them. In fact the only thing he liked more than talking about ghosts was chasing them.

"Spooks?" he would say as he gazed into the fire with his good eye and spat into a nearby cuspidor or anything else that was handy.

"Spooks? Why sure I can tell you about spooks. We got more spooks 'round here than you can shake a stick at!

"Not that shakin' a stick at 'em would do you any good, mind you. No. That would only encourage 'em.

"Apples. What you need is apples. Red ones, green ones, wormy little yellow ones. It don't make no never mind what kind, just so long as you can throw 'em.

"Why's that you ask? Well, I'm gonna tell you. It done knocks then spooks off their guard. Them spooks is so used to people being ascared of 'em that when you throws somethin' at 'em, well, it sorta surprises 'em like; kinda wounds their dignity. Oh, they hate that!

"That's why I always carry a pocket full of apples. Then I'm ready for 'em. All it takes is one good shot. Sure, it sails clean through 'em! But that don't make no never mind. That spook 'ill never bother you again — at least not again that night!"

A visiting skipper with shaggy gray beard would give Welchy a skeptical look.

"I sees you don't believe me," Welchy would respond. "Well, you'll sure believe me once you've spent a night in this place!

"Oh, the tales I could tell you. Like the night somethin' was poundin' like the devil on the front door. You could hear the poundin' all the way to the fourth floor. But when they opened the door, nothin' was there — not even the wind! Well, they closed the door and the bangin' started up again. They opened the door and still there was nothin' there. This happened four times! Nobody knowed what to think.

"Then, later that night, two of me mates were lying in their bunks, jus' chewin' the fat, when the door of their room starts to open, all by itself like. And in floats the skipper of a ship that left port just three months before. Pasty white he was and naked as the day he was born. His hair was wet and matted and you could smell the salt water as it dripped from his skin. A few days later we learned that his ship had gone down with all hands in a typhoon in the Indian Ocean.

"And then there's Tiny Tim. We called him that 'cause he was near seven foot tall. One night he got in a ruckus in some dive on the Barbary Coast and found himself up against a couple of toughs carrying brass knuckles and knives more than a foot long. Well, that was a bit more than he had bargained for and, quick as you can spit, he got his right hand cut plumb off and he was pitched out into the gutter. As he lay there bleedin' to death, he kinda groaned, 'Hey, chuck out me fin, will ya?' To this day, his spirit wanders through these rooms cryin' out those very same words over and over again.

"And, if you go up to the top floor, you jus' might hear the tap, tap, tap of a wooden leg on the floor. You always hear the tap, tap tappin' jus' before you see him. Him, with his swollen face and his peg leg, a walkin' down the hall. He pinches you as he passes. He's a strange one he is!

"But then me favorite stays in the baggage room. It's down there in the basement that we stores the sea chests and the dunnage bags for the sailors before they leave port. Of course, sometimes they never come back. No one goes down there after dark no more — no one, that is, 'cept me! It's 'cause of what happened that night aboard the *Squando*.

"Lets see, now, — it was back in eighty-nine or thereabouts that the *Squando*, a Norwegian bark it was, was tied up here in port. Now, the captain had a right good lookin' wife, 'cept that she had hard eyes — some say evil — but, other than that, she was right good lookin'. And she could be right friendly at times to a lonely sailor, if you catch me drift.

"And there was a first mate on the *Squando* — flamin' red

hair he had — and he took a likin' to her. And she must have takin' a likin' to his red hair or somethin' 'cause she got real friendly with him.

"Well, after they'd gotten real friendly for a few nights, she suddenly started gettin' worried that her husband might find out. You see he was the jealous type and didn't much like to share, if you catch me drift. So she turned Judas on the mate and told her husband that he had been makin' improper advances — botherin' her something fierce. Well, the captain looked right in her purdy face and swallowed every word. And then he got angry — real angry. And he decided to fix it so the mate would never bother her again."

Welchy would then turn away and tend to the fire until one of his listeners would grow impatient and demand, "Well, what happened?"

"That night," he would slowly intone, "the captain invited the mate to his cabin and they got him good and drunk. And when he was too woozy to defend himself, she appeared and held him down while her husband chopped off his head with an axe. Later they found his body a floatin' in the harbor. Never did find his head.

"But that weren't the end of it. For you see, he'd left a chest here in the baggage room. And hidden deep within the chest was a photograph of his unfaithful love. And now, every night, at a certain time, a ghost with flamin' red hair, his face all twisted like, the mark of the axe still on him and the blood oozin' out, appears in the baggage room. He throws open the chest and roots 'round inside till he finds her picture. He pulls it out and stares at it for moment. Then he laughs — a horrible mocking laugh that's as much a cry as a laugh. Then he vanishes as the lid come crashing down.

"That," Welchy would then add with a sly smile, "is why I

never got married. Some women can be real difficult!"

# The Crystal Dress

It was her birthday and it should have been the happiest day of her life but, instead, it was a time of fateful decision for eighteen-year-old Flora Sommerton. The year was 1876. Her father, Charles Benbow Sommerton, was one of the richest men in San Francisco and, in just a few hours, she was to make her debut into the glittering world of the city's most privileged and elite social circle, wearing a beautiful white tulle gown covered throughout with thousands of tiny iridescent hand-sewn crystal beads.

It would be a moment of which most young women could only dream, but all was not as perfect as it might seem. Her parents had decided she would soon marry Hugh Partridge, a man whom she did not love and whom she knew she could never come to love. He was shallow and weak-willed, an arrogant fop known best for an embarrassing nervous laugh and a questionable moral history. He was everything she detested most.

No! She could never marry him but she knew that her mother, bent on using the marriage to elevate even further her own social position, would not be dissuaded. There was only one answer. She would flee her Nob Hill home and all the luxury, privilege and comfort which went with it.

Shortly after lunch she told her mother that she was going out for a walk. With trembling hands she opened the ornate front doors one last time and headed down the hill toward a shop on California Street, a large package carefully wrapped in brown paper tucked tightly under her arm.

Upon reaching the shop, she presented a note she had written and asked a delivery boy to give it to her mother when he made his rounds later that day. He delivered the note to the Sommerton mansion early that evening but everyone so was busy preparing for the debut that the envelope remained unopened until, at last, Flora's mother realized she was missing. Only then did someone remember the note. In a few short, sad lines Flora explained that she could not endure the prospect of marrying Hugh and had determined to make her own way in the world. She had taken with her money and jewelry with which to make a start and asked her parents not to think her "heartless."

Her distraught father and aunt wanted to summon the police immediately. Her mother, however, was made of sterner stuff. She was not going to jeopardize her social standing with a scandal. No, the ball would go on just as planned. They would say Flora had taken ill at the last minute and had been sent away to the country to recuperate. There would be more than enough time the following day to find her — quietly.

The Sommertons brazened their way through the evening and later the next day informed the police of their daughter's disappearance, assuming she would soon turn up unharmed. Flora, however, proved to be far more elusive than anyone could ever have anticipated.

It was soon apparent that she had left the city and, in the months which followed, what would become a world-wide search was begun. A reward of $250,000 was offered for information leading to her return, sparking tips and rumors from across the country. Many of the leads were only the result of wishful thinking but, from time to time, she actually was sighted and the news of her discovery was sent on to San Francisco. Each time, however, she managed to remain one step ahead of her pursuers.

Like many wealthy girls of her day, Flora had been given singing lessons as a part of a proper upbringing and, although she had not been blessed with a professional quality voice, she had hoped that she might at least be able to support herself as a voice teacher. When she surfaced about three years later at a boarding house in Kansas City carrying little in the way of baggage and a large brown paper parcel, she tried her hand at giving voice and piano lessons. She managed to attract a few students but her musical talents were minimal and it was not long before all of her students left her, having realized they could do better elsewhere.

It was about this time that one of her neighbors began to wonder if the music teacher might be the same woman a local newspaper had described as being sought in San Francisco and mentioned her suspicion to Flora's landlady. The landlady informed the police but, before they got back to the house, Flora had vanished in such haste that she had left behind a few of her now meager possessions. She had taken with her, however, the large brown paper parcel.

Years passed and, when the 1906 fire swept across Nob Hill, her parent's mansion burned to the ground. Later, after Flora's father died, her mother called off the detectives, ending the search for their daughter.

It would be years before the next piece of the puzzle would fall into place. It came in the form of a letter from Adele La Blanche, the prima donna in a traveling opera company. While appearing in Chicago a few months before, Miss La Blanche had sprained her ankle and her understudy had to go on in her place. The understudy, however, was more slender than the star and none of her costumes fit. A tired looking middle-aged woman who was serving as a dresser to the women in the chorus suggested that she might be able to help.

The woman went home and brought back a large rumpled and soiled brown paper package. She carefully opened the package to reveal a white tulle evening gown fit for a fairy tale princess. It was covered in dazzling crystal beads and was so stunning that, after recovering, Miss La Blanche asked the dresser if she might purchase it in the hope of having it altered to fit her.

A look of sadness came into the older woman eyes and, for a few moments, she found it difficult to speak. "No, I can't sell it. It is the only link with my past," she explained. "It is Nob Hill and all that I might have been." Then, with a look of panic, she took the dress into her arms and fled from the theater never again to return.

Over the years rumors of Flora Sommerton continued to find their way across the country to San Francisco but in 1916 her mother died and no one but those eager to claim the reward still cared.

In 1926 a woman calling herself Mrs. Butler, who had worked for the last ten years as a maid at the Butte Central Hotel in Butte, Montana, was found dead in her room, the apparent victim of a heart attack. In a nearby valise, the police found a collection of yellowed clippings from newspapers across the country telling of the world-wide search for Flora Sommerton. The woman was found lying on the bed in her bleak hotel room dressed in a white crystal ball gown.

Ever since, the slender figure of a young woman dressed in a white crystal gown has, from time to time, been reported walking slowly up a side street toward the crest of Nob Hill. She smiles wistfully to those who pass by, perchance reliving that day so very long ago on which she made the decision which would change her life forever.

# The Kearney Street Poltergeist

In January of 1866 a young San Francisco newspaper reporter writing under the name of Mark Twain heard about a gang of ferocious ghosts which were said to be wreaking havoc in a home on Kearney Street. He investigated and submitted the following account to the *Territorial Enterprise* in Virginia City.

"Disembodied spirits have been on the rampage now for more than a month past in the house of one Albert Krum, in Kearney Street — so much so that the family finds it impossible to keep a servant forty-eight hours. The moment a new and unsuspecting servant-maid gets fairly to bed and her light blown out, one of those dead and damned scallywags takes her by the hair and just 'hazes' her; grabs her by the waterfall and snakes her out of bed and bounces her on the floor two or three times; other disorderly corpses shy old boots at her head, and bootjacks, and brittle chamber furniture — washbowls, pitchers, hair-oil, teeth brushes, hoop-skirts — anything that comes handy those phantoms seize and hurl at Bridget, and pay no more attention to her howling than if it were music. The spirits tramp, tramp, tramp, about the house at dead of night, and when a light is struck the footsteps cease and the promenader is not visible, and just as soon as the light is out that dead man goes waltzing around again. They are a bloody lot. The young lady of the house was lying in a bed one night with the gas turned down low, when a figure approached her through the gloom, whose ghastly aspect and solemn carriage chilled her to the heart. What do you suppose she did? — jumped up and seized the intruder? — threw a slipper at him? — laid him with a misquotation from Scripture? No — none of these. But with admirable presence of mind she covered up her head and yelled. That is what she did. Few young women would have thought of doing that. The ghost came and stood by the bed and groaned — a deep, agonizing heart-broken groan — and laid a bloody kitten on the pillow by the girl's head. And then it groaned again, and sighed, 'Oh, God, and must it be ?' and bet another bloody kitten. It groaned a third time in sorrow and tribulation, and went one kitten better. And thus the sorrowing spirit stood there, moaning in its anguish and unloading its mewing cargo, until it had stacked up a whole litter of nine little bloody kittens on the girl's pillow, and then, still moaning, moved away and vanished.

"When lights were brought, there were the kittens, with finger marks of bloody hands upon their white fur — the old mother cat, that had come after them, swelled her tail in mortal fear and refused to take hold of them. What do you think of that? What would you think of a ghost that came to your bedside at dead of night and had kittens?"

# The Fatal Prescription

It was long before the earthquake and fire of 1906 that a drama unfolded in a drugstore on Market Street; a tragedy which a druggist named Sweeney would never forget.

"I think I've poisoned someone!" his assistant, Edward Marsden, had stammered; the young man's face frozen in a mask of terror, his complection as pale as death.

"Good God, man, are you certain?" the druggist responded.

"As certain as I can be. About an hour ago a young gentleman came in with a prescription from Dr. Knelligan calling for paregoric. I made up the prescription and sent him off on his way. Only now did I notice the open bottle of salts of lemon out on the laboratory table. I don't know how it could have happened but I must have reached for the wrong bottle and given him salts of lemon rather than paregoric."

"Ring up Dr. Knelligan at once ! Get the man's address and pray you can find him in time," Sweeney ordered.

Marsden immediately proceeded as instructed but, upon reaching the man's home, learned from the landlady that the patient had, just minutes before, left without indicating as to where he might be going.

"When he returns," Marsden gasped, "tell him to not, on

any account, take that prescription!"

Emotionally drained and knowing that his warning would, almost certainly, not be delivered in time, Edward Marsden returned to the pharmacy, informed his employer of his failure to intervene in time and, summoning what little strength remained in him, slowly made his way up the staircase to his room.

Sweeney immediately contacted the police, requesting a city-wide search for the young patient.

Not long thereafter Sweeney, his wife and their servant girl all heard Marsden come downstairs and go out the door. There was no mistaking Marden's heavy manner of walking, his unique "lumping gait."

A few minutes later Sweeney heard a bloodcurdling scream. The maid had gone upstairs to make up Marsden's bed and found, to her horror, Marsden, or rather Marsden's corpse, sitting in a chair, his cold, lifeless eyes staring deep into her soul.

From that moment on Marsden's troubled spirit roamed both the pharmacy and the rooms of the residence above. His heavy footsteps could often be heard day and night, both climbing and descending the staircase to his room.

While mixing prescriptions Sweeney often felt Marsden peering over his shoulder anxiously watching his every move as if attempting to prevent any possible mistake.

One day Mrs. Sweeney thought she saw her husband standing in the parlor. She placed her hand upon his shoulder. The figure she had taken for her husband turned round before her. It was Marsden, his pallid face contorted with despair. The poor woman screamed and Marsden mournfully walked away, passing completely through the servant girl who, having heard her mistress's scream, had, just then, rushed into the room.

"Did you see him?" Mrs. Sweeney excitedly enquired.

"No," the maid replied, "only a dark shadow which seemed to pass before me. But, at that moment, I felt a horrible pang of anguish!"

A week later, both women encountered Marsden on the stairs, passing them so closely that they felt his clothing brushing up against theirs. He appeared so substantial and real that they followed him down into the laboratory. But, upon entering the room, they found it to be entirely empty.

Such phenomena became almost everyday occurrences until, one morning, a young man entered the pharmacy asking for Mr. Sweeney.

"I am told that you have been looking for me," the young man began. "I would have come sooner but I have been out of town for sometime and it wasn't until now that I was contacted by the police. I was the man for whom your assistant filled that prescription. I don't know what he thought might be wrong with it but I drank it as soon as I had arrived home and it helped me immeasurably. I have heard that the poor man's spirit has been seen several times since. Of course, you surely do not believe in such things."

"No, I do not believe in such things," Sweeney replied gravely. "I *know* them to be true."

"Well, if his spirit does linger here, I hope that he now sees that I was unharmed and that he might now rest in peace."

The young man turned and was about to leave when, suddenly, he froze in his tracks.

"Holy Mother of God!" he gasped.

There, standing just outside the shop, his face pressed up against the window, was Edward Marsden; his look of anguish slowly changing first to bewilderment and then to joy and amazement.

Sweeney rushed forward, intending to address him but, just as quickly as it had appeared, the spirit vanished, never to be seen again.

# Broderick

"Gentlemen are you ready?" a voice rang out through the morning air as Senator David C. Broderick nervously tried to adjust the stock of the unusual Belgian dueling pistol to somehow fit the contour of his hand. He had never seen such a weapon before and realized at once that he was at a serious disadvantage. He had been ill for days and had not been able to sleep the previous night. Standing ten paces away, with the cool confidence of one who knows the outcome before the contest has even begun, Judge David S. Terry calmly replied, "Ready."

Suddenly life seemed very precious to the senator — the touch of the morning sun on the ocean waves as they crashed onto the shore, the scent of the morning air after a gentle spring rain; the song of a bird, the warmth of a friend's smile. Each of these simple joys and so many other small miracles of the common day which he never before seemed to have had the time to fully appreciate now possessed value beyond measure. But it was all too late. He, who had so masterfully controlled his entire life and the lives of so many others, was no longer in command of his own destiny. He was, at last, only an actor in the tragic concluding scene of his own life drama. The last act had already been written and he now had no choice but to speak the lines fate had decreed. Slowly he pulled his soft black hat down low over his forehead, and answered, "Ready."

It seemed impossible that it should all end here. In thirty-nine short years he had come so far and he might have, one day, risen so high as to win the White House. But now, it seemed, his enemies had triumphed at last.

Born February 4, 1820 in the District of Columbia, the son of a stone-cutter who had helped shape the marble columns which now grace the eastern facade of the Capitol, David C. Broderick was, in the words of Gertrude Atherton, "ambition incarnate". He was only fourteen when his father had died and, as an apprentice stone-cutter, he had taken on the responsibility of supporting his mother and brother. His family had moved to New York and, as soon as he was old enough, Broderick joined the New York Volunteer Fire Department where he quickly became known for both his courage and his ability to end any dispute with his fists. He was soon made foreman of his fire company and eagerly entered into the rough and tumble world of Tammany Hall politics.

He opened two saloons which attracted the neighborhood politicians and both his political and his economic fortunes quickly increased. When he was twenty-four his mother and brother died and, perhaps to fill the void left in his life, Broderick immersed himself entirely in politics. He helped presidential candidate, James Polk, carry New York and became a force with which to be reckoned. But he had also made many enemies along the way among both the Whigs and the aristocratic leadership of his own Democratic party. When he ran for Congress, the heads of both parties conspired to ensure his defeat.

Then gold was discovered in California. Broderick decided that his star had risen in the west and he left New York vowing he would, one day, return east as a United States senator.

He arrived in San Francisco on June 13, 1849 weakened and ill from disease contracted during a stay on the Isthmus of Panama prior to the final leg of his journey. But within a month he had recovered and, with a friend from New York, he established an assay office and began minting five and ten dollar gold pieces containing significantly less gold than their stated value.

Following the city's first major fire, Broderick organized a fire fighting company and, through it, began his career in San Francisco politics. After only six months in the city, he was elected to California's first state legislature, rapidly creating a political machine which would soon control almost every aspect of city government. When such positions as sheriff, district attorney, tax collector or alderman came up for election, any aspirant had to first strike a deal with Broderick. Although many of these positions carried no salaries, the official was expected to take home a certain percentage of the fees and fines collected by his office. This made some offices worth as much as fifty thousand dollars a year. The worth of each office was carefully appraised and Broderick would be promised half. In return, Broderick arranged for the candidate to receive the Democratic party's nomination and guaranteed his election. In the years which followed, this arrangement funneled several hundred thousand dollars a year into Broderick's pockets. Finally his control over the Democratic Party became such that, in 1857, he was sent by the state legislature to the United States Senate.

Despite being corrupt and utterly ruthless as a politician, Broderick maintained and was scrupulously faithful to some deeply held principles. Chief among them was an undying opposition to the spread of slavery. This was a dangerous view in parts of California in the 1850's as transplanted Southerners wielded a great deal of influence in the Democratic Party.

Undaunted, Broderick became a leader in the fight to prevent the extension of slavery into western states, incurring the wrath of both President Buchanan and large segments of his own party. A naturally charismatic leader who could easily command the love and support of a crowd, he was seen in some quarters as an extremely dangerous man who had to be stopped at all costs.

When Congress adjourned in 1859, Broderick returned to California to wage a vigorous home state campaign against the spread of slavery into Kansas. At the Democratic Party's state convention, a fiery southerner, David S. Terry, then Chief Justice of the California Supreme Court, delivered a speech thoroughly denouncing Broderick.

A few days later, while having breakfast at the International Hotel, Broderick read an account of the speech and was outraged. Speaking to a friend, he recalled how he had spent several hundred dollars to defend Terry when, only three years before, the latter had been held prisoner by the Second Committee of Vigilance. "I have said that I considered him the only honorable man on the Supreme bench," Broderick lamented, "but now I take it all back."

His conversation was overheard by a friend of Terry's who took offense and challenged the senator to a duel. Broderick, who had survived a number of duels and was considered to be a crack shot, replied that he would only accept such a challenge from "a gentleman holding a position equally elevated and responsible" and then only after the conclusion of the September election.

The friend relayed word of all that had transpired to Judge Terry who vowed to issue a formal challenge immediately following the election. Terry would have over two months in which to carefully plot his strategy and he would use his time wisely.

Terry had not had much experience with firearms. His weapon of choice was the Bowie knife which he always carried and used with deadly skill. But he knew Broderick would demand pistols and sought advice from a Dr. Aylette of Stockton who was known to be an expert on the subject of dueling pistols. Dr. Aylette was pleased to provide not only advice but a pair of Belgian dueling pistols as well. Although their barrels were a standard twelve inches in length, the construction of the stock was considerably different from that of the standard American dueling pistol. More importantly, one of the pair had a hair trigger so delicate that the pistol fired as the result of any quick movement or jarring of the weapon. Although the other of the pair also had a light trigger, it was, by comparison with its mate, almost normal in its action. In a duel two years earlier, a man given the especially sensitive weapon, despite having practiced with it, failed twice to raise the pistol even slightly without firing his bullet into the ground just a little in front of him and, on a third try, succeeded only in raising it as high as his opponent's knee before the weapon discharged.

When Terry first attempted to fire Aylette's pistols he was quite literally unable to hit the broad side of a barn. Under the doctor's tutelage, however, he quickly became an expert marksman.

By election day, September 7, 1859, Terry was ready. The next day, he began an exchange of formal notes requiring that the senator retract "any words which were calculated to reflect on my character as an official or a gentleman." When Broderick refused to do so, Terry demanded "the satisfaction usual among gentlemen."

Broderick had been ill for several days, perhaps with pneumonia, and was staying at the Black Point home of a friend, Leonidas Haskell, on the edge of what is now Fort Mason. But as the duel was to occur early in the morning, ten miles away, on the shore of Lake Merced, Broderick, in the company of a surgeon and his seconds, spent the night before in a miserable little inn near the lake. Their bedding consisted of hard cots lacking in adequate coverings and infested with sand fleas. None of them were able to get any sleep and the next morning, September 14, 1859, Broderick arrived at the site of the duel without having had breakfast or even a warm cup of coffee. Terry had spent the previous evening comfortably in a cozy bed nearby and had enjoyed a hearty breakfast.

By the time the men met, at around six in the morning, a crowd of approximately seventy-five spectators had arrived to view the proceedings. A somber fog brooded over the battlefield. After the tossing of a fifty-cent piece, Broderick's seconds won the choice of position and the giving of the word to fire but Terry's seconds won the choice of weapons. A local gunsmith had brought a pair of pistols never before used by either party. Terry had brought the Aylette pistols and his seconds chose them. They should have tossed the coin again to determine which of the chosen pair would go to which party but one of Terry's seconds quickly picked up one of the pistols, leaving the other for the senator.

Standing too far away to know for certain that his opponent had received the faulty weapon, Terry appeared agitated and worried as the pistols were loaded and the distance measured out. Then one of his seconds whispered something to him. He then smiled and wore about him a calm, cool air of confidence.

The duelists discarded their overcoats and took up their positions at about a quarter to seven. As each man answered "Ready," he lowered his weapon to his side, the barrel pointing toward the ground. For a moment all was eerily quiet.

Then the command to fire rang out. As Broderick started to raise his hand, his pistol fired, the ball plunging into the earth a few feet away. He looked down at it with surprise as Terry raised his pistol, took deliberate aim and fired directly at Broderick's heart.

The senator felt a fierce blow to the chest as the bullet struck him a little above the right breast, traveled through his body and lodged itself in his left shoulder. He tried to brace himself and remain standing but he soon began to turn and stagger and then, slowly, he dropped to the ground, blood flowing from his chest. Only then did the pistol fall from his hand.

As Broderick's surgeon rushed to the senator's side, a saw ominously extending from his bag, Judge Terry coldly commented, "The wound is not mortal. I have hit two inches too far out." Broderick had earlier told his friends that he had no real animosity toward Terry and would not aim above his waist.

Broderick's physician quickly became confused and panic-stricken and Terry's surgeon gallantly took over. They were unable to remove the lead ball and, fearing the worst, had him driven back over ten miles of rough road to Haskell's home where he lingered for three days suffering from convulsions, every breath being difficult, as the best physicians in San Francisco struggled to save his life.

Battling the inevitable, Broderick spoke in a feeble voice of the principles for which he had fought in the Senate. "They have killed me," he said, "because I was opposed to a corrupt administration and the extension of slavery."

His fight for life ended on the morning of September 16, 1859. His last words were, "I die. Protect my honor."

San Francisco was cast into mourning. Strong men cried on the street and hardheaded businessmen closed their offices and draped their doorways in black. For two days an air of depression hung about the city as Broderick's body lay in state at the Union Hotel. On Sunday, September 18 his body was placed on a catafalque in Portsmouth Plaza where thirty thousand mourners gathered for his funeral. It has been said that almost the entire male population of San Francisco followed the coffin to its destination at the foot of Lone Mountain Cemetery.

But while his mortal remains were interred in the Lone Mountain Cemetery, it seems his troubled spirit may have remained at the Haskell House for, over the years, the beautiful home still standing high above the bay has been the scene of otherwise unexplainable happenings. High ranking army officers billeted in the house during the Army's period of residence at Fort Mason and not given to flights of fancy have reported such eerie phenomena as lights which flicker on and off with no apparent reason, a bedroom door which refuses to stay closed, flower arrangements destroyed by unseen hands, areas in the house in which the hair on one's arm stands up on end as if in an electrical field, the disquieting feeling of an unseen presence and the sound of someone walking upstairs when no one is there.

Some claim to have heard Senator Broderick's mournful voice in the darkness while others have actually seen him. It is always the same. He appears on the steps of the house, makes his way down the walk and then vanishes into a cluster of trees. He is dressed as he was the morning of the duel in a long frock coat, a white shirt and a broad black hat. The front of his shirt is stained with blood.

# The Faithful Chorister

It was almost ten o'clock that Friday morning in August of 1890 when Edwin Russell felt a blinding bolt of pain flood across his brow. Everything went dark as he collapsed onto the pavement near the corner of Sutter and Mason Streets and, within an hour, the fifty-year-old real estate agent was dead of a cerebral hemorrhage.

A transplanted Englishman who had lived in San Francisco for ten years, Russell had a wonderfully resonate bass singing voice and was greatly appreciated at St. Luke's Episcopal Church where he had long been a faithful and dependable member of the choir. When the wife of St. Luke's rector heard about Russell's death, she sent her brother, a Mr. Sprague, to the home of Harry E. Reeves, St. Luke's choirmaster, to inform him of Russell's death and to ask him to begin choosing music for the funeral.

When Sprague arrived that afternoon at Reeves' 2121 California Street residence, he was met by the choirmaster's sister and niece. They welcomed him in, explaining that Reeves was upstairs. The choirmaster had been going over two *Te Deum*s, trying to decide which piece of music to use the following Sunday, when he heard the doorbell ring. Knowing his sister would call him if he was needed, he had decided to lie down and rest for a moment in his bedroom.

But upon closing his eyes, he was seized by an inexplicable impulse to rise and go to the bedroom door. When he opened the door, he saw Russell standing there before him, holding one hand to his forehead and gesturing with a rolled up sheet of music in the other hand. The image was so clear and lifelike that the choirmaster reached out his hand to greet him and was about to speak when the figure turned away, slowly dissolving into the air. Reeves attempted to call out to his friend but became momentarily paralyzed and fell back against the wall. "My God!" he finally exclaimed.

Upon hearing his words, Sprague and the others rushed upstairs where they found him sitting on the staircase, frightened and confused. "I've just seen Russell," he started to explain.

"But that's impossible," his niece interrupted. "Mr. Sprague just told us that Mr. Russell died this morning."

The blood drained from the choirmaster's face. Slowly he rose to his feet and, without another word, went back upstairs to his room. Only then did he relate to them the details of what he had seen.

Perhaps it had merely been a case of clairvoyance. Perhaps Reeves had psychically become aware of Russell's death and his mind had, somehow, manufactured an hallucination which might have brought that knowledge into consciousness. But then, perhaps, it was something more. Perhaps the faithful chorister had felt so strongly about his obligation to the choir that, even after death, he had returned to let the choirmaster know that he would be unable to sing on Sunday.

# Duncan's Castle

Rising gracefully from the summit of Telegraph Hill, standing cool and aloof, stately and patrician, like an elegant dowager surveying her estate, Coit Tower gazes serenely down upon the city below. It seems as if she has always been there but the fact is that the aristocratic sentinel is a relative newcomer to a spot upon which flocks of goats once grazed and early San Franciscans once gathered to watch men on horseback hack away at each other with deadly sabers.

It all began in 1850 when a marine telegraph was constructed at the top of what forevermore would be known as Telegraph Hill. A semaphore station, it was a small two-story house built around a tall, sturdy mast from which two wooden arms could be arranged to announce in code what kind of ship had been sighted entering the harbor. Two men lived continuously in the station house, keeping watch for ships, setting the semaphores and serving simple refreshments to anyone adventurous enough to climb to the top of the hill for a visit.

The station was a great success but soon fell victim to progress when, in 1853, the construction of an electric telegraph service made the semaphore obsolete. A telescope was then installed through which anyone with twenty-five cents to spare could enjoy a spectacular view of the entire Bay Area. And a friendly bartender was also on hand to reward sightseers with liquid fortification.

Again the Telegraph Hill outpost was a great success and thousands of hardy souls made the exhausting climb, commemorating their feat by carving their names into the clapboard siding of the building. It all came to an abrupt end, however, in the early hours of December 7, 1870 when a violent southeaster quickly reduced the station house to firewood and the debris was almost as quickly carted away by neighbors intent on utilizing it to warm their homes.

For over a decade the summit of Telegraph Hill stood bare until, in the spring of 1882, Frederick O. Layman, an enterprising real estate man, began the construction of an enormous Victorian castle-like structure which would serve as both an observatory and a resort. He also began what would become a two year struggle to build a cable car line which could safely transport the anticipated crowds up the hill.

At last, on Sunday, June 29, 1884, all was in readiness and both the cable car line and the castle were opened for business amidst great fanfare and celebration. Although from two to three thousand spectators attended the opening day festivities, the observatory's success was short-lived and the property soon became a white elephant.

Then the extraordinary figure of Duncan C. Ross strode onto the scene. Ross, a handsome, muscular Scotsman who stood a little over six feet in height and weighed two hundred and thirty pounds, had an idea. A former instructor of swordsmanship with the Royal Scots Greys, Ross had, in 1880, defeated a Texas Ranger in a mounted broadsword exhibition in Louisville, Kentucky and again emerged victorious when a similar contest was staged in San Francisco in 1885. Eighteen hundred spectators had come to see what was billed as an "assault at arms" and an impresario was born.

Ross took possession of what was now being called "Layman's Folly" and the castle became the ideal stage upon which Ross, as lord of the manor and local champion, took on all challengers. He leveled out a forty-by-fifty foot area below one corner of the castle to form an arena and, almost every Sunday, several thousand onlookers crowded the terraces and parapets of the castle to watch him meet his latest opponent in a twenty-nine round bout.

To the cheers of the crowd, two men would enter the arena where they were ceremoniously clad in a crudely fashioned version of medieval armor, their mounts straining at the bit in anticipation. First, each man buckled on sheet metal breastplates and backplates weighing altogether approximately ten pounds and then donned a neckplate of steel and a heavily padded and specially reinforced fencing mask with two heavy wires running down the back to the shoulders to protect the nape of the neck. Wristlets of heavy leather and a hard leather guard for the upper arm protected the sword arm. In addition, a leather wristlet was usually worn on the bridle arm. Ross fearlessly wore no hand or arm protection other than the wristlet on his sword arm; a daring move as the swords — regulation cavalry sabers — though dulled at the point, were otherwise razor sharp.

Once mounted, the combatants charged into the fray, each attempting to strike the other on the chest or back, receiving one point for each successful assault. A hit below the armor or to an opponent's horse (which carried no armor) resulted in the loss of a point, while a blow to the head, though not considered a foul, yielded no points. If a swordsman was thrown from his horse, he was expected to finish the round on foot.

Although the armor did provide some protection, the battles were not for the squeamish nor the faint of heart. In a match with Sergeant Charles Walsh, (a veteran of Sherman's march on Atlanta, the winner of eleven exhibitions of swordsmanship in Mexico and the only challenger to ever defeat Ross) Ross slashed his saber into Walsh's shoulder only to have Walsh reply with a blow to Ross's face so fierce that the wire mask gave way and Ross was cut on the chin. In a bout with Captain E. W. Jennings, an ex-British officer, Ross inflicted a four inch gash to the skull when his opponent's helmet slipped. Ross had tried to pull back the blow as he saw helmet fall but it was too late and Jennings narrowly escaped being killed. Such accidents were not unusual and it was a rare match that ended without bloodshed.

For over a year, Ross defeated all other challengers from an Australian policeman to an Italian tamale peddler who fought under the name of "Garibaldi" and he added such variations as taking on an opponent armed with musket and bayonet. But the public finally grew tired of the knightly contests and, at last, Ross reluctantly passed the keys to his proud castle into other hands.

In the years which followed, the once proud castle fell into disrepair and gradually became known as a "hoodlum resort." At one time plans were announced to restore the observatory to its former glory but they never got beyond the talking stage. Windows fell from their frames and bats flew through the empty halls of the abandoned and decaying castle.

It was during this time that a workman told of spending a night in the ruins of the former barroom. He had fallen asleep on an old packing crate only to be awakened by horrible piercing shrieks. Two disembodied skulls radiating a sickening blue light and screaming out a torrent of curses hovered in the darkness above him. It was said that these phantoms, which had haunted other homes on the western slope of Telegraph Hill, were the spirits of a man and his wife who had, in times gone by, been cheated out of their home on the hill and were then murdered.

Sometime later, the castle was sold to The Gray Brothers Crushed Rock Company who used the old building as barracks for their workmen. But strange things continued to happen. It was said that men disappeared in the castle, never to be seen again. During the waning of the moon, bloody footprints were to be found on the flagstone flooring although no mortal form had trod upon them. And the spectral form of a growling black dog was often seen to run in and out of the castle only to vanish whenever it was confronted.

Finally, on the morning of July 25, 1903, the castle burst into flames as two frightened little boys quickly fled down the hill. Six horses struggled to pull Engine No. 5 up the steep grade to the castle and hundreds of volunteers helped carry hoses up the hill but, despite everyone's best efforts, Duncan's Castle was soon reduced to a blazing memory. Like the semaphore station before it, the last remaining fragments of the castle were quickly carted away by the neighbors for firewood and, again, the summit of Telegraph Hill was left sadly barren. Or was it?

It would be almost three decades before construction would begin on Coit Tower and, during those years, on clear moonlit nights from time to time, something could be seen by local residents standing at the top of the hill; a pale, solitary figure gazing out toward the bay.

Some said it was the ghost of Sergeant José Ortega who, as chief scout for Don Gaspar de Portola, was the first European to cast his eyes upon San Francisco Bay. Perhaps, they theorized, he had returned to preserve his rightful claim and to protest historians who credited his discovery to Portola, who had actually been ten miles away and had probably been asleep at the time or, worse still, credited his discovery to the English privateer, Sir Francis Drake! Others said it was the ghost of Duncan Ross waiting to take on new challengers.

# Ghosts of the Golden Gate

Ghostly ships with phantom crews, tattered sails and tortured rigging have long been said to haunt the seas; the endless wail of spectral seamen echoing across the waves. It is hardly surprising, then, that the port of San Francisco, with the rich legacy of its seafaring past, should have its share of ghost ships.

Perhaps the earliest reported ship said to haunt the Golden Gate is the *Tennessee*, a phantom clipper which has often been sighted just outside the bay, speeding under full sail toward the safety of port, only to vanish upon reaching Lime Point. She then rematerializes amid patches of fog further out to sea where, once more, the *Tennessee* attempts her futile journey home.

Then there was the strange occurrence aboard the *U.S.S. Kennison*. In November 1942, the old Navy destroyer was carefully threading its way through a treacherous fog northwest off the Farallone Islands when suddenly the fantail lookout, Torpedoman First Class Jack Cornelius, saw something incredible. A rotting two-masted sailing ship slowly emerged from out of the fog and headed toward the *Kennison*, almost colliding into her. It drifted to within a few yards of the fantail and remained in view for twenty to thirty seconds. Cornelius was able to observe the strange craft closely. Her deck was weathered, her sails and rigging torn and the last traces of paint had long since peeled away. But most incredible of all, her decks were deserted and her wheel unmanned. As he watched spellbound, the sailor was seized by an eerie, uncomfortable feeling.

He lunged for the controls of his headphone and shouted to Tripod, the fire control man standing watch on the after gun deck, "Look aft!"

"My God, Jack!" Tripod answered back. "I see something but what is it?"

That was a question which would be repeated for many months aboard the *Kennison*. It could not have been an hallucination. A third sailor, Howard H. Brisbane, who had been standing watch on the galley deck at the time, reported clearly hearing the bow wash of the ghost ship and the creaking of her timbers and rigging. And though the radar man had been carefully monitoring his scope for the approach of the Farallones, not a trace of the ship had been picked up on radar.

A ghost ship of a far different kind was the British square-rigger *Blairmore*, which sailed into San Francisco in February of 1896 with a cargo of Welsh coal for the J.D. Spreckels & Brothers sugar refinery. Her captain, John Caw, had hoped to pick up a grain charter to replace the coal but as the market was then quite slow he discharged all but a skeleton crew. For well over a month his ship lay at anchor in the bay south of the Ferry Building, her hull empty of all but her standing ballast, riding dangerously high in the water.

At 6:40 on the morning of April 9th, a squall began to brew out of the southeast while a flood tide grasped the *Blairmore* from the opposite direction causing her to heel over to one side. Captain Caw, the cook, carpenter and watchman were all above deck at the time. The remaining eleven men, however, were below chipping rust from the ship's hold. Seeing the danger, the *Active*, a nearby tug towing another ship into port, let go of its charge and raced to the *Blairmore*'s side. Captain Caw, however, either too concerned about potential salvage claims by the tug or failing to appreciate the danger, as the ship had by now righted itself, declined the *Active*'s offer of assistance. Most of the crew, however, had previously expressed the fear that the ship was not carrying enough ballast and might capsize in bad weather. Those below had all made a mad rush for the deck when the ship started to sway. But now all seemed calm and the men apprehensively went back down below while the captain set about straightening up some flower pots which had slid about the deck.

Fifteen minutes later, a howling second squall hit the *Blairmore* full on the port side with such force that, for an instant, she was lifted up entirely out of the water, throwing her masts starboard in an horrifying arc and plunging her spars into the sea. Her keel began to rise from the water. Back and forth the ship rolled as if in a desperate attempt to right herself. But water was now flooding into her open hatchways and slowly the great ship began to sink.

Captain Caw, on the poop deck when the ship started to overturn, was thrown overboard along with his dog, a collie named Jack. Swimming to the surface, he saw Jack, grabbed him and together they swam to the safety of a longboat tied to the ship's stern. Unable to pull himself inside the boat, he desperately clung to its side, the weight of his body partially supported by the struggling dog.

The ship's carpenter, James Watson, jumped from the ship and swam to the longboat, soon followed by the third mate, William Melville.

Not everyone, however, was so fortunate. First Mate Thomas Ludgate, Second Mate Dougal McDonald and nine crewmen were in the hold when the second squall hit. As the ship started to roll, Ludgate jumped from an eight foot high scaffolding, staggered to his feet and yelled, "For God's sake, boys, get out!" A moment later he was hit by a wall of flying debris and knocked to the floor. Fighting the torrent of freezing salt water which was pouring down into the hold, the crew frantically ran up a ladder to the hatch. As Ludgate tried to make it through the hatch he was again struck, this time by a floating capstan-bar, and thrown back into the hold. An apprentice seaman was hit in the head by a wooden plank and, along with Ludgate and two others, was trapped in the hold as the ship turned over.

Almost immediately, the air echoed with the sound of alarm whistles as rescue boats were quickly launched from every ship anchored in the bay. Within minutes Captain Caw and Jack were rescued by a crew from another British ship while the carpenter and third mate freed the *Blairmore*'s longboat and set out in search of their shipmates. Not long after, the second mate and three others who had escaped from the hold were found clinging to the side of the sinking ship. Two others were pulled from the water where they clung to the ship's rudder. At the same time crews from four other ships and six tugs searched in vain for any remaining survivors.

As the ship turned over enough air had been trapped in the hold to keep the *Blairmore* afloat. Rescuers circling the ship heard a hammering from within the hold and the voices of at least two of the imprisoned sailors. An attempt was made by a tugboat to pull the *Blairmore* back up and, perhaps, tow her into port. But the weight of the ship and the water she had taken on were too much for the tug and the effort had to be abandoned.

Something had to be done to rescue the men still alive in the hold. Superintendent James Dickie of the Union Iron Works shipyard soon arrived with a number of his men and it was decided that a hole should be cut in the side of the ship directly above the place where the voices had been heard. Soundings were taken and, after comparing them with an estimate of the *Blairmore*'s width, Dickie incorrectly concluded that the ship was safely resting on the mud of the bay floor. He carefully climbed onto the ship's side and began tapping on the iron hull with a hammer. Hearing the sound of voices from within, he ordered his men to begin cutting out a twenty-two by twenty-six inch section. By now the tide was rising quickly and his men were in such danger of being swept off the hull that they had to be secured with ropes tied to the ship's railing. In the superintendent's words, "It was a race between man and the tide."

For an hour and a half, while the men inside cheered them on, the cutters worked under miserable conditions, made worse by the ever-rising tide. By the time the rescuers were about to strike the final blows which would free the plate, the ship was submerged under half an inch of water.

No sooner was the final cut made than a powerful geyser of compressed air and water shot up out of the hole twenty feet into the air. The iron workers were thrown back by the blinding column of salt water. Attempting to shield themselves with their coats, they tried to fight their way back to the opening they had made but the savage blast of water and air was too much for them. The ship quickly filled with water and disappeared beneath the waves.

"We heard the voices of the men up to within four minutes of the time we made an opening into the hold," Superintendent

Dickie later stated. "They were congregated around the place where we were working ready to spring out. Had we got there an hour sooner, we would have saved them."

About three months later the *Blairmore* was patched sufficiently to be raised up from the bay floor, pumped out and towed to the nearby Pacific Rolling Mills wharf where she would remain while her owners decided her ultimate fate. The bodies of those who had died within her iron hull were found and given a proper burial.

This, however, was not to be the end of the story. Perhaps the men who had died aboard her had signed on for eternity; for soon strange stories were being told along the waterfront.

Night watchmen reported seeing mysterious lights floating about the *Blairmore*'s brine soaked decks and hearing equally inexplicable sounds issuing from deep within her hold — a ceaseless pounding on the side of the hull and an ominous deep rumbling sound like that of shifting ballast. It was not long before Pacific Rolling Mills was having difficulty retaining night watchmen.

They did find one man, however, for whom ghosts held no terror. While on watch one night, he began to hear eerie sounds echoing from within the *Blairmore* and he decided to investigate. Fearlessly, he climbed onto the ship and looked down into the opening of the main hatch. Though he could see nothing, the ghostly banging continued on in the darkness. He slowly lowered his lantern down into the hold, suspending it from a length of string. The sounds stopped. Cautiously, he ventured down into the hold. No one was to be seen. He shrugged and climbed back up the ladder.

Almost immediately the pounding resumed and the watchman fled the ship in horror.

After a while the haunting became so well known that a

spiritualist decided to visit the ship one night. He later reported feeling his neck "encircled by ghostly arms" and his hands "clasped by invisible spirits" and he claimed to have been given a message from beyond the grave by one of the drowned sailors.

Finally, over the next few months, the ghostly noises seemed to diminish until, at last, they ceased entirely and, if any ghosts were still aboard, they would soon have to share their quarters with the living for the ship was repaired, refitted, rechristened and sent out to sea again under the name, the *Abbey Palmer*.

A few years later she was sold to the Alaska Packers Association of San Francisco, becoming a sister ship to San Francisco's *Balclutha* and San Diego's *Star of India* and, in 1906, by a special act of Congress, her name was again changed, this time to the *Star of England*.

While her sister ships were to end their careers in glory as floating memorials to the past, the *Blairmore* was not fated to be so fortunate. When the days of the great sailing ships were past, she was renamed one last time, her masts cut down, and, as the *Island Star*, served as a humble sawdust barge in British Columbia until, on a misty day in 1962, she was sold for scrap and quietly faded into history.

In her last hours her fo'c'sle head capstan was rescued from the shipbreakers and is now on display on the *Balclutha*.

# The House of Mystery

Lightning flashed and a howling wind drove the rain hard against the arched bay windows of the uninhabited three story mansion with the blood red mansard roof which then stood at the corner of Bush and Octavia as Mike, the night watchman, made his way down a path winding through the remains of the once proud garden. Unexpectedly, he heard two doors open and then violently shut. A vague, dark form sped past him. It was a cold night but, just the same, Mike felt something even colder briefly touch his arm. He turned to look down the path, but whatever it was had vanished. As he walked toward the house, he again saw the dark figure rush past him, stopping, at last, before the front door where it turned and motioned to him as if enjoining him to follow.

As Mike drew nearer, he could see the figure more clearly. A tall, elderly woman, stately and aristocratic in bearing, beckoned to him with a commanding hand, her white, starched neckerchief standing out in stark contrast to her black dress and dusky skin. Her hair was pulled back tightly in a patrician manner, her gold earrings glistening in the darkness. He knew instantly it was "Mammy" Pleasant, the mysterious woman who had, decades before, built the mansion he now guarded. But that was impossible. She had died in 1904 and Mike was not one to believe in ghosts. Surely, someone was playing a practical joke.

He was not about to be run off by a prankster, however, and Mike headed toward her, cautiously climbing the six stone steps leading up to the home's imposing front entry. But just as he reached the top step, the strange figure suddenly dissolved into nothingness. Bewildered, Mike tried to peer through the etched glass windows set deeply within ornately carved double doors. He perceived only darkness.

Then one of the doors slowly opened, as if by itself. Mrs. Pleasant stood there before him, her eyes glowing with an unearthly fire. Now Mike was frightened. He tried to leave but some horrible power held him within its grasp. As if in a trance, he followed her into the house through the fifty foot long entry hall in which Italian frescoes brooded like shadows upon the walls and down a staircase which led to the basement.

Mike stopped and tried to turn back but the old woman forced him onward with a hypnotic motion of her long slender fingers, laughing and saying, as if to herself, "There are reasons. There are reasons!" Despite the fear which grew more intense with each step he took, the watchman was powerless to do anything but follow. And although each of his footsteps echoed ominously throughout the cavernous old house, the steps of his guide never made a sound.

When they reached the basement, she pried loose a plank from the floor and began digging into the earth below with her bare fingers until, at last, she reached the object of her search and pulled from out of the soil a crucifix to which a medal emblazoned with a Masonic symbol had been tied. Holding it out toward him, she said, "Take it. You'll need it!" Then, with a hideous scream, she vanished as the crucifix fell to Mike's feet.

Mike was to often speak of that night in the years which followed and, often, those to whom he told his story would laugh and call him a liar. But then he would grimly smile and produce the proof which he always carried with him, an earth-encrusted Masonic medal tied to a weathered crucifix.

Mike was not alone in having experienced the chillingly unexplainable in the house which had even before Mary Ellen Pleasant's death been known as the "House of Mystery." Doors in the house were said to open and close by themselves throughout night, candles carried by those brave enough to explore the deserted mansion were inexplicably snuffed out and many had seen the ghost of the proud old woman standing beneath the eucalyptus trees which she, herself, had planted so many years before.

A ghost hunter who once dared to spend a night in the house described seeing a spectral form which sighed mournfully as it slowly strode through the empty ballroom. A few moments later, a deadly thud was heard at the bottom of the grand staircase. In death, as in life, people would speak in hushed tones of "Mammy" Pleasant and the house only she could have built.

Mary Ellen Pleasant — some called her an angel. Others called her a demon and worse. Like most of us, however, she was a curious mixture of both, a fearless champion for the rights of her fellow African-Americans and a ruthless businesswoman who let nothing stand in the way of bringing her schemes to fruition — a figure worthy of Shakespeare who, but for a tragic flaw born, perhaps, of the prejudice and injustice of her time, might have achieved a greatness of heroic proportions. We will never know the whole truth. By now fact and fantasy, envy and fear, gossip and prejudice, have become so tightly bound together that it is impossible to ever separate one from the other and to know, for certain, which parts of her story are true and which are merely legend. The following narrative of her life is based upon the "facts," as best we know them, as recalled by those who knew her but who may have had their own reasons to distort the truth or totally invent malicious lies. Thus, the reader must judge the possible validity of those "facts" for him or herself. Unfortunately, the few who actually knew the truth long ago took that knowledge with them to their graves.

She was born, it is said, in 1814, a slave on a plantation in Georgia and given the name Mary. Her mother, being of only one-quarter African heritage, had unusually light colored skin and claimed descent from a long line of voodoo queens in her native Santo Domingo. Her father was a prosperous plantation owner from Virginia.

When Mary was only ten years old, her mother was sold and sent away, never to be seen by her again. But, in those ten short years, her mother must have instilled in the young girl a fierce belief in herself and a pride in her heritage which not only helped her endure the pain of separation but would give her strength and direction throughout her entire life.

Then one day a miracle occurred. Americus Price, a wealthy planter from Missouri rode by the plantation in need of directions to town. He was impressed by Mary's intelligence and promptly arranged to purchase her. Instead of taking her to his plantation, however, he secretly sent the young girl, who was light enough in complexion to pass for Spanish or Creole, to a New Orleans convent where she was to be given an education.

She was an excellent student and made the most of the opportunity until, a short time later, her patron died and Mary was again sold, this time as a bond servant, to the owner of a general store in Nantucket, Massachusetts.

The store owner, whom everyone called "Grandma," was as kind as her nickname would suggest and when, years later, her period of bondage had expired, Mary stayed on of her own free will to care for the then elderly lady whom she had come to love.

When Mary was twenty-four, "Grandma" died. For the first time in her life, Mary Ellen, as she now called herself, was truly free to do whatever she wished and she moved to Boston where she obtained employment as a seamstress and soon embarked on a cooly calculated scheme to attract and marry James W. Smith, a wealthy merchant with sizable investments and a plantation in Virginia. She did not love him. She had not, yet, even met him. But that was not important. In three weeks time, Mary Ellen stood before the alter with her first conquest.

Marriage, however, held an unexpected and most welcome surprise. Her new husband was an ardent abolitionist who ran his plantation entirely with a paid workforce of former slaves whom he had bought and then immediately freed. It was not long before they were both deeply involved in the dangerous business of helping slaves escape to the safety of Canada by way of the Underground Railroad.

In 1844 James Smith fell fatally ill. On his deathbed, he asked Mary Ellen to use his fortune to continue the fight against slavery. She needed no encouragement and spent the next eight years sending slaves to freedom through the Underground Railroad, boldly keeping just one step ahead of her pursuers and depleting her fortune in the process.

She became so successful that slave holders began to place a high priority on her capture. She was a master of disguise. Sometimes she would appear at a plantation as a deliveryman. Other times she would assume the identity of a jockey. She taught herself to become an superb cook and landed a position presiding over the kitchen of a plantation on the outskirts of New Orleans.

Unfortunately, this time she had somewhat overplayed her hand and, when her employer began to brag about his wonderful new cook, one of his friends became suspicious that the extraordinary cook might be the very woman for whom they had been searching. Mary Ellen overheard the man's conjecture and quickly booked passage on a ship bound for San Francisco.

Upon arriving in San Francisco on the 7th of April, 1852, she was amazed to find a number of men waiting at the dock waving fistfuls of currency in her direction. Word had preceded her arrival that she was the best cook in New Orleans and men long starved for culinary talent in the rough and tumble new city began to bid for her services. She carefully appraised the various offers and, a week later, accepted the position of housekeeper at a boarding house catering to eight prosperous bachelors with the understanding that she would merely supervise a staff of her own choosing and not have to perform any of the actual work herself.

Under Mary Ellen's masterful direction, the boarding house became not just a comfortable home but an oasis of elegance and refinement in a city desperately lacking in both and an invitation to dine at her table became a highly coveted prize.

She shrewdly invested her salary in the rapidly growing city; building first a laundry, which was soon followed by two more. She next added a livery stable and a saloon. In the years which followed, she would move on to oversee other exclusive boarding houses where she would discreetly eavesdrop on the conversations of the powerful men who flocked to her establishments, gleaning invaluable inside information which she then artfully utilized in the volatile financial markets of the time to quickly multiply the proceeds flowing from her various enterprises.

A large percentage of her income she used to pay the cost of sending newly escaped slaves to San Francisco. Once there, she found the former slaves shelter and employment and zealously protected them from any who might attempt to seize them and return them to a life of bondage. Later in life she proudly claimed to have financially supported John Brown's ill fated raid on Harpers Ferry.

Following the Civil War, she struck an early blow for racial equality by suing a San Francisco bus company with the claim that she had been denied passage on a bus because she was black. Everyone knew the charge was merely a pretext for litigation. She always had a carriage available to her from her livery stable and, consequently, never took the bus. That, however, did not matter. She had made her point and never again would any member of her race be denied the use of public transportation in the city of San Francisco.

She multiplied her financial holdings with increased devotion and, at the same time, it is said, began weaving a web in which she hoped, one day, to ensnare the most powerful men in San Francisco. A pivotal player in this plan was Thomas Bell, a young Scotsman she had first met on her voyage to San Francisco. When she encounterted him again four years later, he had obtained a modest position with an investment banking firm and seemed the ideal person to handle Mary Ellen's investment portfolio. At first Bell tried to offer advice but he soon learned that his client had not come seeking his counsel. She always knew exactly what investments she wished to make and, to his amazement, her judgment proved almost always infallible. To the outside world she was merely a highly desirable housekeeper. Within the small circle of the city's financial elite, however, she became known as an extremely shrewd investor.

She continued to add to her already impressive real estate holdings. By 1868 she owned three boarding houses. Two were unpretentious, built to attract the middle and lower echelon employees of the financial district. The third, at 920 Washington Street, however, was elegantly appointed and hosted such powerful men as William Chapman Ralston, Darius Ogden Mills and William Sharon, the financial titans behind the Bank of California. At the boarding houses she and her staff eavesdropped on private conversations, gathering the inside information necessary for her speculations in the financial markets. Eventually the task would be made easier when a secret passage with listening posts for each room was installed in the Washington Street house.

Always looking to maximize profits, Mary Ellen torn down one of her laundries and replaced it with a discreetly run brothel. When this enterprise proved successful, she demolished a second laundry and built an opulent "house" modeled after one she had seen in New Orleans. She had hoped to lure the same powerful men who dined at her boarding house table to these new establishments but, disappointingly, few were tempted.

Finally, the last of her laundries was torn down and there, at the then remote and secluded corner of Geneva and San Jose Roads, she built an intimate and elegant retreat within which she planned evenings so exotic and forbidden that her quarry would surely succumb and fall into her increasingly merciless grasp.

At what became known as the Geneva Cottage, Mary Ellen was said to have offered something special for parties limited to ten men chosen from among city's elite. They would enjoy a perfect dinner and the finest of wines in the company of ten ravishingly beautiful woman elegantly clothed in exquisite low-cut evening gowns accented with simple but perfectly chosen jewels. The refined young ladies were all protégées of Mary Ellen, women she had rescued from the streets and carefully trained to tease and charm their partners into marrying them. Thus, her charges would, one day, preside over the finest San Francisco families and Mary Ellen would hold power over them by knowing the secrets of their past.

It was later whispered that Mary Ellen would invite back the more adventurous of her patrons, always in groups of ten, to the cottage to experience something they could find nowhere else. Waiting for them would be ten beautiful black women with whom they would drink and dance to the beat of an African drum, participating in what she claimed to be an authentic voodoo ritual. These saturnalias always culminated in the full satisfaction of her patrons' sexual desires. For these forbidden pleasures, the men would pay her handsomely — first at the time of their indiscretion and then, again, later, to have the memory of their evenings at the cottage remain a secret.

By now, through following Mary Ellen's investment tips, Thomas Bell had become a wealthy and powerful man in his own right and, at the Geneva Cottage one night, he found himself seated beside a bewitchingly lovely young woman with long golden curls and enchantingly deep blue eyes. Her name was Teresa Percy.

Over the years Mary Ellen had placed hundreds of her devoted followers into the homes of the most the city's most prominent families as servants. There they would learn their employer's secrets and report back to the always curious Mrs. Pleasant. When the unmarried daughter of a wealthy socialite found herself in the embarrassing position of producing an unwelcome heir, the always helpful Mrs. Pleasant could be counted on to whisk the girl away to a house she kept for just such emergencies. And, when the time came, she could always find "a more suitable" home for the child. Soon, slowly savoring each word, Mary Ellen would be able to boast "I hold the key to every closet in town with a skeleton in it."

But Mary Ellen did not need to resort to blackmail or salacious schemes to achieve wealth and power. She had made millions in entirely legitimate enterprises and, by the fall of 1875, when many of the city's financial speculators were ruined by a devastating stock market crash, she and her silent partner, Thomas Bell, had accumulated over thirty million dollars.

Perhaps she enjoyed conjuring up elaborate schemes, luring her victims into skillfully spun webs of intrigue. Perhaps she took a cruel pleasure in outwitting and then destroying her prey. If so, it would be that very same love of intrigue and deception which would ultimately lead to her own downfall.

For reasons known only to herself, Mary Ellen, who now called herself Mary Ellen Pleasant, attempted to hide her assets by recording them in the names of silent partners. The fruits of her stock market speculations were held in the name of Thomas Bell while most of her real estate was recorded in the name of her most important protégée, Teresa Percy, who had dutifully signed, along with anything Mrs. Pleasant might require, a document giving Mary Ellen her power of attorney.

At first Teresa complied out of gratitude for Mary Ellen's having taken her in and furnishing her with every luxury. Later she complied out of fear.

Mary Ellen knew that Teresa had an estranged husband who had come to San Francisco in search of her. She convinced Teresa that her life was in danger, gave her a pistol and coached her in its use until she had became highly proficient with the weapon. Mary Ellen then informed the enraged husband as to when and where he might find his errant wife. When he arrived, his pistol drawn, Teresa hesitated. Mary Ellen yelled out to her, "Fire!" and in front of Thomas Bell and two other witnesses, Teresa shot her husband through the head. It was clearly a case of self-defense and, if it had been immediately reported, Mary Ellen would have had no hold on her. But, almost immediately, one of Mary Ellen's most trusted employees appeared, as if from nowhere, and set to work quietly removing the body and cleaning away any remaining evidence. The dearly departed was buried in one of the forty-nine plots in the Laurel Hill Cemetery which, it was whispered, Mary Ellen held for just such occasions.

Mary Ellen's hold over Thomas Bell came much easier. She had discovered that he was a wanted man, sought back in England by Scotland Yard.

Once she had total control over the leading players in the drama to come, Mary Ellen set about creating a proper stage upon which her actors might perform, speaking only those lines she would give them. She obtained a lot, exactly one-half block in size, fronting on Octavia Street and stretching between Sutter and Bush Streets and built a house measuring ninety feet wide by one hundred and thirty feet long. It rose to three stories with a full basement and was nothing short of palatial. Italian frescoes graced baronial sized rooms lit with rock crystal chandeliers. Gilded mirrors reflected the glow of fireplaces surmounted with carved marble mantels.

In Mary Ellen's bedroom cupids and classical nudes painted on the fifteen foot high ceiling gazed down upon a sumptuous gilded French bed and walls lined with eight life-sized portraits of nude women and eight mirrors of the same size, all hung in gilded frames. Over her bedroom fireplace hung a portrait of Thomas Bell. Behind one of the mirrors was a secret passageway providing access to both a tunnel ending a hundred feet or so away in the carriage house and a maze of four-foot wide passageways running between the walls through which she could eavesdrop on almost every room in the house. Part of the basement, it was rumored, was used for voodoo rites.

In September, 1878 she moved Teresa into the new house along with two small children whom Mary Ellen had deceived Thomas Bell into believing were his own by another of her protégées. She also duped the public into believing he had secretly married Teresa by listing her as Mrs. Teresa Bell in the city directory.

Mary Ellen had never really desired that Bell marry Teresa or anyone else, for a wife would become his legal heir. But Teresa misunderstood her intentions and one night lured Bell to the house. After inducing him to drink an entire bottle of one of Mary Ellen's highly potent alcoholic concoctions, she led him into the drawing room where a waiting priest conducted a marriage ceremony. The next day an enraged Thomas Bell fled San Francisco, not to be seen again for seven months.

Upon his return, Mary Ellen persuaded the reluctant newlywed into accepting the inevitable and he moved into the Octavia Street mansion where "Mr. and Mrs. Bell" lived in separate apartments, rarely saw each other and even more rarely spoke to one another. This was perfectly fine with Mary Ellen. She had only desired the appearance of marital bliss. For it was later disclosed that she was more than just Thomas Bell's financial partner and advisor. She was also his lover.

At last the stage was set and all the players in place. Mary Ellen was now ready to use the wealth and power she had accumulated to take her place as an equal among the elite of San Francisco society and she hoped that, by doing so, the other members of her race would also be looked upon as equals by their white peers. She was on the threshold of fulfilling her greatest desire.

But she had waited too long. Most of her protégées had, by this time, left San Francisco. The friends of Thomas Bell would always treat Mary Ellen with a combination of fear and respect but, with arrival of the railroad barons and the Comstock "Silver Kings," there came a new aristocracy over whom she had no control. The new elite saw her only as an embarrassing vestige of San Francisco's past; a past best forgotten. Six years later, her financial empire began to crumble. Most of Thomas Bell and Mary Ellen's assets were invested in a company engaged in hydraulic mining, the rest were in mines producing the mercury vital to extracting gold from its ore. When, in 1884, hydraulic mining was outlawed, a major source of income dried up. With the end of hydraulic mining, the value of mercury also plummeted.

Nevertheless, Mary Ellen continued to spend as if she had unlimited resources and, whenever possible, on credit. Her unpaid dry-goods bills alone totaled over forty thousand dollars.

Thomas Bell attempted to bolster his sagging fortune through reckless stock speculation using money borrowed against his few remaining assets. Years before Mary Ellen would have guided his investments and warned him of potential pitfalls but now she had no time for his problems. She had become heavily involved in one last desperate attempt to win back millions.

A beautiful woman named Sarah Althea Hill had become intimately involved with Senator William Sharon, an unscrupulous financial manipulator who had made millions from the Comstock mines and ruined his friend and benefactor, William Chapman Ralston, in the process. The senator had offered Miss Hill five hundred dollars a month to become his mistress but she was not to be so easily bought and persuaded Sharon into signing a legally binding marriage contract.

When the senator later tired of her and moved on to new conquests, Miss Hill turned to Mary Ellen for help. Numerous and sometimes grisly Voodoo charms were said to have been tried in an attempt to win back his affections but all to no avail. Finally Allie Hill filed suit for divorce requesting one-half of Sharon's thirty million dollar estate. Sharon contested the action, claiming Allie had merely been his mistress and that the marriage contract was a forgery.

Mary Ellen secretly paid not only the staggering expense of the divorce proceedings but also the cost of the never ending array of dazzling and exquisitely chosen dresses, coats and bonnets which Allie Hill wore at the trial. In return, if Miss Hill prevailed in court, Mary Ellen would receive one half of the expected award.

Legal costs alone mounted to at least a thousand dollars a day and the almost endless parade of one hundred and eleven witnesses caused the trial to rage on for more than six months. Mary Ellen needed cash to feed the ravenous legal monster she had created and there was almost nothing she would not do to obtain it.

When she learned that a black waiter who owned a valuable piece of Berkeley real estate was having marital difficulties, she talked him into hiding his assets by temporarily signing the property over to her until his divorce was finalized. She promised to later give him a secret deed of reconveyance. When, following his divorce, she continually failed to return the deed, the waiter began to worry. He heard rumors that Mary Ellen had stolen property from other member of her own race. Almost hysterical, he ordered her to return the title to his property. Mary Ellen never flinched. She calmly agreed to meet him in Oakland, where she claimed to have left his deed. The next day the man's body was found floating in the Oakland Estuary.

The Sharon trial took more than just a financial toll. For months its scandalous revelations became the city's favorite source of entertainment, a seemingly endless drama more spellbinding than the most lurid novel could provide, as, one by one, closely guarded secrets of what had become known as the "House of Mystery" on Octavia Street were brought out into the harsh light of day. Shocking stories of black magic filled the columns of the city's newspapers and Mary Ellen Pleasant, benefactor of the poor and the oppressed, became known as "Mammy" Pleasant, a chilling, evil force, corrupting all she touched.

The term "Mammy" particularly rankled her. Although she allowed close friends to use the term and, perhaps, even enjoyed being so addressed by those who used it as a term of endearment, she found its use by others to be insulting in the extreme.

"I don't like to be called Mammy by everybody," she once snapped to a reporter. "Put that down. I'm not Mammy to everybody in California.

"I got a letter today from a minister in Sacramento. It was addressed to Mammy Pleasant. I wrote back to him on his own paper that my name was Mrs. Mary E. Pleasant.

"I wouldn't waste any of my paper on him. The letter wasn't in the house fifteen minutes. I sent it right back to him unread.

"Between you and me, I don't care anything about it, but they shan't do it. They shan't nickname me at my age! If he didn't have better sense he should have had better manners..."

For a moment, however, it seemed worth all the sacrifice when the trial judge declared the marital contract valid and awarded Sarah Althea one-half of the senator's assets. But then, after expending still another fortune on numerous appeals and related court actions which dragged on for over five years, the original ruling was overturned. It had all been for nothing.

Meanwhile everything was rapidly unraveling on Octavia Street. Mary Ellen had been forced to heavily mortgage most of her properties during the years squandered in court and, while her legitimate sources of income were providing less and less with each successive year, her expenses were as great as ever. Thomas Bell had seriously over-extended himself and, if not stopped, might lose all that was left. Somehow Mary Ellen had to regain control.

She knew that Bell had written a will leaving everything to Teresa but had named Mary Ellen as administrator. In that capacity she would have complete control of his estate. What she did not know was that in 1892 he had written a new will providing for the children. But, more importantly, to thwart Mary Ellen, he had named three of his friends as executors. Mary Ellen was to be left nothing.

On October 15, 1892, Mary Ellen overheard a telephone conversation in which Bell instructed his attorney to come by the next day to make yet another change to his will. Not knowing the real damage had already been done, Mary Ellen decided to act.

That evening she brought a bottle of warmed wine up to Bell's bedroom. The wine had been drugged. Later that night, after the servants had retired to their rooms, she silently stole into his room, an accomplice by her side. Together they carried the unconscious Bell from his room and stood him near the top of the carved walnut spiral staircase. She gazed wistfully upon her lover's face one last time and then whispered, "Throw him over."

Her accomplice suddenly panicked and fled. Mary Ellen glared in anger, hoisted Bell into her arms and hurled him over the railing.

"Mammy, where am I?" Bell cried out as he hit the parquet floor below.

One of the maids ran into the hallway just in time to see Mary Ellen bending over Bell's quivering body, gouging her fingers into a gash in his skull.

The servant kept the horror of all she had seen to herself for years and Thomas Bell was officially found to have suffered from an accidental fall. Perhaps, it was suggested, he had become confused and made a wrong turn on his way to the water closet.

When the will was read, Mary Ellen learned the terrible truth. Bell's estate would not be divided until the youngest of the children reached the age of twenty-one. Until then the executors would be allowed to do whatever they wished with the assets. Fearing that two of the executors would quickly steal whatever they could, the third man quickly resigned his appointment.

The ominous prediction proved correct and, while Teresa was given a token allowance, the remaining two executors set about hiding many of Bell's assets and selling the remainder to themselves at prices reflecting only a small fraction of their true value.

With each day, life on Octavia Street became more and more a nightmare. The two older children attempted to kill Teresa by tying a rope across a tread near the top of the staircase where she might trip and fall. At the same time, the eldest son began stealing from Mary Ellen who quickly struck back, firing a few pistol shots at him and later pushing him down a darkened staircase.

Unable to afford proper upkeep, the "House of Mystery" began to deteriorate. Rain trickled down through cracked plaster ceilings onto the floors of unheated rooms while Mary Ellen, sensing the end was near, spirited away the remaining silver, furniture and anything else of value.

Then, on October 24, 1898, Teresa learned the last witness to the shooting of her first husband had died. No longer could Mary Ellen hold the threat of a murder charge over her. Months earlier Teresa had found the power of attorney she had signed years before as well as incriminating documents in which Mary Ellen had, strangely enough, kept a meticulous accounting of her many crimes. Teresa had destroyed the power of attorney and hid Mary Ellen's secret papers, waiting for the day which, finally, had arrived. At last she would be free of the woman who, for over thirty years, had controlled almost every aspect of her life.

For several months she continued to endure Mary Ellen's icy presence as she made plans to put the house up for sale. Then she learned that Mary Ellen had helped the youngest child steal and melt down the last of Teresa's gold jewelry. She could take the strain no longer. She threw Mary Ellen's few remaining possessions into a gunny sack and demanded that the frail old woman leave the house immediately.

Mary Ellen barricaded herself within her rooms and sent for her lawyer. After examining the deed to the house, which she had, years before, signed over to Teresa, her lawyer explained that there was nothing he could do. The next morning a large crowd gathered to watch the spectacle of the eighty-three-year-old Mary Ellen Pleasant leaving, for the last time, the strange house only she could have built.

For four years Mary Ellen had been slowly wasting away from cold and hunger in a cheerless, filthy apartment when a newspaper reporter offered her fifty thousand dollars if she would divulge the secrets through which she had once held an entire city in silent fear. For a moment her sad eyes flashed in anger. "I have never needed money badly enough," she proudly replied, "to betray a friend."

A few months later, an acquaintance found her so weak that she could no longer move from her bed. She took the old woman to her own home where, on January 11th, 1904, Mary Ellen Pleasant sank into the welcoming embrace of death.

Over the years, the "House of Mystery" continued to deteriorate until, in 1926, it was demolished. After thoroughly searching the grounds for a box of diamonds Mary Ellen was rumored to have secretly buried on the property, the new owner erected an L-shaped hospital just behind and flanking the previous site of the "House of Mystery." The shape and positioning of the hospital merely reflected a revolutionary new style of hospital architecture. Uncharitable neighbors, however, suggested that Mary Ellen had cursed the house as she left it for the last time and, rather than risk her wrath, the new owner had thought it only prudent to build around the place where her home had once stood.

Whatever the truth may be, it is said that ghosts often linger long after the home in which they lived has faded into memory, opening doors no longer there and prowling dark halls seen only through ghostly eyes. And when the fog filters through the limbs of the giant eucalyptus trees which still brood over the sidewalk at 1661 Octavia Street and a cool breeze gently whispers through their leaves, passers-by who tarry too long beneath the trees might still glimpse a tall, dark figure who beckons with an imperious gesture and, perhaps, find reason to believe that Mary Ellen Pleasant still presides over the "House of Mystery."

# The Phantom Parishioner

Perhaps it is the serenity to be found within the its Norman-Romanesque walls erected in 1892 along the lines of Durham Cathedral in England. Perhaps it is the light filtering softly through its stained glass windows or the music swelling from the towering pipes of its magnificent organ. Perhaps we shall never know. What we do know is that something has caused a mysterious phantom to remain within the grey stone confines of Trinity Episcopal Church at the corner of Gough and Bush.

Roger LaClear-Zangaro, who served as the church sexton for over a decade has come to know the phantom well. One evening, while vacuuming near the altar, Roger was astonished to see what he later described as "a three dimensional shadow of a human figure" descend the steps from the altar and then pass close by him.

One Sunday, shortly after everyone had departed following the 8:00 AM service, Roger was again vacuuming when he suddenly felt the hair stand up on the back of his neck. Turning around, he saw "a tall slender figure wearing an off-white linen suit" standing in the section of pews across the aisle. "He was standing there facing me," Roger remembered "and as I started to focus on his face he vanished right before my eyes. I was not startled this time because I sensed the figure was not trying to frighten me."

On yet another occasion he had been pushing all the kneelers back under the pews. "When I walked down the middle aisle," he recounted, "I was checking that all the kneelers were in straight rows. About halfway down the church in one of the rows, one of the kneelers was pushed out from the rest of the kneelers. This kneeler looks different from all the rest and is sort of an oddball kneeler and I distinctly remembered pushing that kneeler under the pew. I was startled by what I saw but I went over and pushed it back underneath the pew. No one else was in the Sanctuary with me, and Paul, the other sexton, was cleaning the rooms downstairs at the time."

Once, at around ten in the evening, while mopping one of the restrooms in the ambulatory, Roger suddenly heard what seemed to be the footsteps of a man walking down the hallway. As the footsteps drew nearer, he stopped mopping and looked out into the hall. No one was to be seen, though the ghostly footsteps continued on past him and down the hallway. For a few moments he felt "frozen stiff," unable to move, his hair again standing on end until, at last, he was able to break free of the phantom's spell, throw down his mop and flee down the backstairs yelling for Paul.

Sometimes, when alone in the men's restroom downstairs, Roger was unable to shake the eerie feeling that someone was watching him. And it is here that parishioners have observed a man who would suddenly vanish before their eyes and it is in the hall, just outside this restroom, that a number of others have observed a gray shadow-like figure.

One evening Roger and Paul were giving their neighbor, Andy, a tour of the church when suddenly their guest cried out in surprise, "What was that?" Although the specter had vanished before Roger had a chance to look, the neighbor described seeing a "gray shadowy looking figure" standing near the men's restroom door. Andy had not heard about the ghost before.

Even stranger phenomena was to occur in the future. "It was about 2 AM on a dark winter morning," Roger recounts, "while I was mopping the wood floor in the dining room, that a bright glow of light appeared. My eyes were looking on the floor as I was mopping when this glow of light began brightening the room. The room appeared as it would during daylight hours. Thinking that this might be a power surge to the several wall sconces in the room I looked up only to see that the glow was not coming from the sconces. I glanced at the windows only to realize that the light was not shining in from outside. Then, as I turned to look towards the middle of the room, a roundish pulsating form of glowing light was hovering slowly approximately eight feet high from the floor and thirty feet from where I was standing. After five to seven seconds the form darted out through a set of side doors that were opened to the hallway. It then darted through the hallway as I saw it pass another set of opened doors down through the corridor towards a small staircase that leads to another hallway where the restrooms are located. I just stood there holding my mop in amazement and trying to comprehend what had just happened. Just a few feet from where I was standing when all of this was happening is a large closet-room that holds some of the church's archives. Below the floor lies the crypt of the first rector, Rev. Flavel Mines. I've always wondered if that could've been him."

Late one afternoon, just as the sun was setting, Roger decided to take a break and play a one-fingered tune on the church's E. M. Skinner pipe organ. "While I was toodling with the organ. I felt a presence close behind me. The only way I can describe it," he explained, is for one to sit down in a chair sometime and "have someone slowly approach you from behind and have them extend their hands slowly beside and about five or six inches from each ear. While this is being done don't move and look straight ahead until you feel the feeling of someone behind you. The hair begins to stand up on the back of your neck and arms. Well, I took a deep breath and slowly got off the organ bench and turned off the organ. I did not see or hear anything but I wondered afterwards if it was the gray entity that I had seen before."

On another occasion, while volunteering his services at a church luncheon, "I went to the pantry room and suddenly the light went off. I flipped the switch back and forth and the lights came on. I though nothing of it and figured it was a short in the wire. A few minutes later I went to the pantry again and once more the lights went off. Again I flipped the light switch back and forth and the lights came back on. I thought how odd that this happened twice. I called one of the other volunteers and told him that it seemed the lights in the pantry go out whenever I go in there. This time he went with me and sure enough, the lights went out again. Since that time, there has never been any problem with the lights in the pantry room."

More recently two kitchen workers helping with a church program providing lunchtime meals for the elderly quit after only a few days on the job when one of them saw a gray shadowy form emerge from the men's restroom only to pass through a wall on the other side of the hallway. On a separate occasion, the second worker observed the same figure near the entrance to the kitchen. Both workers were deaf and had no previous knowledge of the ghostly phenomena associated with the church.

Two ladies who assist with Trinity's "Meals on Wheels" program and open up the kitchen and diningroom in the morning have both described seeing the ghostly form of a man in the dining room and in the main hallway and refuse to enter the building alone. Instead, each waits for the other to arrive so that they may face together whatever may lurk inside.

Roger feels, however, that there is nothing to fear. He is inclined to believe that the ghost is a harmless, timid soul who prefers to remain hidden in dark, quiet areas of the church. Perhaps, he merely wishes, in his own quiet way, to remain a part of the church community.

# The Atherton Mansion

There stands on the northeast corner of California and Octavia Streets an enchanting souvenir of that bygone era when sleek carriages leisurely wended their way through the city streets delivering jeweled, gloved and elegantly gowned women and their dashing companions to the doorsteps of magnificent homes where they would dance in dazzling ballrooms to the strains of Straus waltzes. Known as the Atherton Mansion, it is a quixotic combination of Queen Anne, Stick-Eastlake and other styles of architecture. Boasting a storybook gable, dormer windows, columns, carved capitals and a fanciful rounded tower crowned with a tall, conical "witch's hat" roof, this unique Victorian concoction was built in 1881 for Dominga de Goni Atherton, the widow of Faxon Dean Atherton, a pillar of early San Francisco society.

In the days of his adventurous youth, Faxon had left his native New England for Valparaiso, Chile where, in the 1830's, he had made his fortune shipping tallow and hides to the East Coast and, later, married Dominga, a member of the wealthy de Goni family. Following the gold rush, Faxon had foreseen the future importance of the city of San Francisco and began shipping food stuffs and other goods there, investing his profits in California real estate. Around the year 1860, he, his wife and their six children moved to California. They lived for a short time on Rincon Hill and then moved to an impressive estate in San Mateo County which he christened Valparaiso Park, at what is now known as the city of Atherton.

Like their contemporaries living on spacious country estates on the peninsula, the Athertons enjoyed comfortable lives based on rules firmly grounded upon time-honored and unalterable tradition. The men regularly left their homes in the morning to conduct business in San Francisco and felt quite free to remain there overnight should the demands of business or other prerogatives of their gender require an extended stay in the city. The women remained at home tending to the children, supervising the servants and, in general, doing their best to make things comfortable for their men.

Into this orderly, predictable world came Gertrude Horn who, in a moment of weakness, had married George, one of the Atherton sons. Gertrude did not love George but he had proposed so many times that it had finally seemed best to just marry him and get the whole thing over and done with. Besides, it had seemed rather like an episode from a romantic novel when, without warning and armed only with the marriage license in his pocket, he had whisked her away in his carriage to an awaiting priest.

Life with George at Valparaiso Park, however, was anything but romantic. It was boring. True, she had almost every luxury and servants at the ready to tend to her every desire but nothing very exciting ever seemed to happen. And, most of all, she missed the companionship of books. Always before she had been able to escape the troubles of the common day by immersing herself in the magic to be found only in books. Even as a child Gertrude had been a voracious reader, constantly demanding that the Mechanic's Library order the latest books for her. By the time she was eight, she had become infamous for storming into the library where, with a look of urgency, she would ask, "Have you got my new book, and, if not, why not?" But books were not to be found in the Atherton home. Senora Atherton curtly explained that, in her culture, well-bred ladies did not read.

Adding to Gertrude's difficulties was the fact that, although George had a good heart and eagerly devoted himself to each new enterprise that came along, he had failed at everything he attempted. His father had set him up in a brokerage house but the results were disastrous. He twice tried his hand at ranching but failed at that as well. These failures served only to weaken further an already shaky marriage. Gertrude, who had expected her husband to be the invincible hero from a novel by Sir Walter Scott, would later call him "a mere male, nothing more."

George was as unhappy as Gertrude and would become even more unhappy when Gertrude's first novel, *The Randolphs of the Redwoods* was serialized in the San Francisco magazine, *The Argonaut*. "Well-bred ladies do not write," Dominga informed her daughter-in-law. But even more unforgivable was the fact that Gertrude had based her novel upon a true story which had shocked the local aristocracy some years earlier. One of their circle was an alcoholic who had laced her baby daughter's food with small amounts of whiskey, gradually increasing the dosage day by day until the child would consume nothing which did not contain alcohol. Eventually the child became an alcoholic as well. Although Gertrude had changed all the names and had drawn a great deal from her own imagination, she had depicted members of the peninsula's finest families, including her own sister-in-law, with such precision that they were easily recognized by all who read her novel. And the novel gained such notoriety that even the most well-bred ladies eagerly read *The Randolphs of the Redwoods*. After a while the storm subsided but there would be some who would refuse to ever speak to Gertrude Atherton again.

A few years before this, Faxon had died and Dominga decided the time had come to escape the seclusion of the peninsula from time to time. She needed a home in the city and built the house on California Street. It was there that Gertrude would see George for the last time.

One day the Chilean man-of-war *Pilcomayo* sailed into San Francisco Bay under the command of Senora Atherton's nephew, Alberto de Goni, and Dominga gave a ball at the California Street mansion in honor of the ship's officers. It was a glittering affair in a house perfectly suited to the occasion. Beautiful women in silk gowns with sweeping full skirts and bustles danced in the grand ballroom while other guests enjoyed the festivities from a gallery lining the second floor. Gertrude, independent as ever, would not wear a traditional ball gown. Instead she appeared in a unique creation of fine white camel's hair which, in her own words, "fitted every part of me like a glove and ended in long train." Dark blue asters accented her waist line. Senora Atherton was to say with consternation, "Very pretty, but not the dress for a ball. Why you no can be like anyone else? What you do next I wonder? Poor George!"

When a few days later poor George hesitantly mentioned that Captain de Goni had invited him to be his guest on the voyage back to Chile, Gertrude was delighted by the thought of months free from George and by now she had learned exactly how to handle her husband. She pretended to vehemently oppose the trip. "If you have any pride," she goaded him, "you will stay here in San Francisco and make something of yourself!" Her plan worked perfectly and, within a matter of days, George set sail on the *Pilcomayo*.

A few months later Gertrude read in a newspaper that the "embalmed remains of George Atherton" had arrived in port on the schooner *Tropic Bird*. It seems that poor George was destined to fail at everything — even at taking a vacation. After only two weeks on board the *Pilcomayo*, George had died of complications from a kidney stone and, rather than bury him at sea, Captain de Goni had thoughtfully preserved the body by doubling it up and plunging it into a barrel of rum. The barrel was kept in the hold until they reached Tahiti. There, under the cover of night, the barrel was secretly placed on board the *Tropic Bird*. Since carrying a corpse was considered bad luck by sailors, it was hidden under a pile of coconuts. In due time the barrel reached San Francisco followed three days later by a letter relating, in tortured English, the details of George's death. It stated that when his "remnants" were placed in the rum "the sailors grumbled, for it came out of their rations" and politely suggested that it would be most appreciated if Mrs. Atherton "made it up to them."

Gertrude later wrote, "I had an uneasy idea that George would haunt me if he could" and, perhaps, he tried. However, she was not going to wait around to find out. She quickly packed her bags and, with a small allowance from the Atherton estate, set out for New York to pursue what was to become a distinguished literary career.

After Dominga's death in 1890, the California Street house was sold and the property passed through a number of hands until it was purchased in 1923 by Charles J. Rousseau, an architect who lived directly across the street. Rousseau subdivided the house into thirteen separate apartments. Years later, his widow moved into one of them. Although she never had children, when she died in 1974 at the age of ninety-three, Mrs. Rousseau left behind a collection of beautifully fashioned baby clothes and forty-five cats.

It was at about this time that stories began to circulate about a ghostly resident in the house. From time to time, at around midnight, phosphorescent lights could be seen darting about the mansion, always to be followed by unexplainable, childlike banging in the attic. Other times it manifested itself as a sudden "rush of wind." One resident reported often being awakened by an eerie knocking at her door just after she had fallen asleep. And a gentleman living in the tower room was to become extremely annoyed by the incessant pounding on his ceiling and what he mysteriously referred to as "the materializations."

Dick Swan, a salesman living in what had been the billiard room, felt the ghost became unusually upset when Mrs. Rousseau died. "You could feel an intense psychic commotion as Mrs. Rousseau's spirit left the house," he related several weeks later. "The pipes broke and, after that, the refrigerator units blew and the furnace boiler went out and my phone is still nothing but static."

It has been suggested by some that, considering George Atherton's long history of failure and the inability of the ghost to materialize clearly enough to be recognized, much less actually frighten anyone, the ghost might be that of poor George Atherton. Sad to say, they might be right.

# Joaquin Murrieta

It was late one night in March of 1853 when a Mexican ranchero heard a loud knocking at the door of his hacienda on the Salinas plains and a voice demanding admittance. He was not expecting guests and it was rare for anyone to arrive in the dead of night but, cautiously, he opened the door.

Standing before him were three Mexican horsemen holding the reins of the finest horses the man had ever seen. Their leader was a tall, handsome man of about twenty-one years wearing a beard and what appeared to be a false moustache. He also wore about him four revolvers and a large Bowie knife. His companions were similarly well armed. The young man explained that they had become lost on their way south to purchase cattle and politely asked if they might beg some refreshment before traveling on.

The ranchero was concerned for the welfare of his family but, upon observing his visitors' weaponry, he felt there was even greater danger in denying them entrance. After some hesitation, he offered them the hospitality of his home.

As his wife served them a hearty supper, the horsemen politely conversed with their hosts on a number of topics and, gradually, the ranchero grew suspicious that the mysterious young man sitting across the table from him might be the infamous Joaquin Murrieta who, according the newspapers, had terrorized the mining camps of the gold country. He was far too wise, however, to broach the question directly, so he merely asked if his guests had heard any news of the celebrated bandit.

The young man looked deep into his host's eyes, placed his hand over his heart and said gravely, "I, Senor, am that Joaquin." Then, quietly, and with an air of sadness, he told his story.

"I was once a great admirer of the Americanos and thought them to be the most generous, noble and liberal people in the world. I had known so many of them in my own country, men of the most honorable principles, men who hated tyranny and injustice. I left Mexico to escape the revolutions and insecurity of my homeland and came here to earn my own way and end my days in peace as a citizen of the country I so admired.

"With an American friend, I took up a piece of land, not far from Stockton, and was getting a fine little farm under way when I was annoyed and insulted in the most vile manner and injured to such a degree by my neighbors that I could no longer live in peace and had to leave.

"Then I went into the placers and was getting on very well until I was robbed of forty thousand dollars, flogged and driven from my claim by lawless miners.

"I next went into business and trade but was swindled and cheated by everyone I trusted." Suddenly he became very excited. "This," he said, "from the very people for whom I had the greatest friendship and admiration! Daily, I saw them commit acts of the most outrageous and lawless injustice and of the most hateful and mean duplicity."

He became very quiet, looked away for a moment and then continued in a pensive and deliberate manner. "I said to myself,

I will avenge my wrongs. I will take the law into my own hands. Those who have injured me, I will slay. Those who have not, I'll rob. In my tracks there will be a trail of blood and he that seeks me shall lie in the dust. Never again will I submit to such humiliation! I will get back what has been taken from me and many times over or I will die in the struggle."

"But what about the danger?" the ranchero asked. "There's a great reward on your head!"

The young man smiled and recalled, as if savoring a precious memory, how he had once heard that a large reward was being offered for his capture, dead or alive. "I rode into Stockton in disguise," he told his hosts as they listened spellbound. "I walked freely about town reading the handbills posted here and there. Finally I found one offering five thousand dollars for my arrest. I wrote underneath: 'I, myself, will give ten thousand dollars — Joaquin.' So long as I have these good weapons, no man will take me alive or even come within one hundred yards of me!"

Shortly after midnight, Joaquin and his companions paid for their meal, graciously thanked their hosts and disappeared into the night.

This much we may assume to be true for it was recorded at the time by the Monterey correspondent to the *San Francisco Daily Herald*. Unfortunately, however, most of the story of early California's most celebrated outlaw will forever remain shrouded in mystery. It was said that during the two months in which he plundered Amador, Calaveras and Mariposa counties, he and his band killed between twenty-four to twenty-nine men, stole hundreds of horses and a fortune in cash and gold. It was said that he was an eloquent, well educated young man from a fine family who, before taking to a life of crime, had been quiet, modest and possessed of an honorable character. But it has also been said that he was a vicious, brutal killer who stole not only from the Americanos but from his fellow Mexicans as well and, often, from the most oppressed and defenseless group of all in the southern mines, the Chinese.

What was he really? We shall never know. At the time of his activities, almost every crime thought to be committed by a Mexican was attributed to him, even crimes committed on the same day and hundreds of miles apart! Not only could no one agree as to a detailed description of the fearless outlaw but he was given at least five different last names by his pursuers.

There was, however, one thing everyone agreed upon. He was a most extraordinary and elusive foe. Beset by five different posses at the same time, Joaquin, a magnificent horseman, always managed to escape capture. The story is told of how, when identified in a gambling hall in Fiddletown, he sprang up onto a table, waved his revolver above his head and shouted, "Yes, I am Joaquin and I defy any man to take me dead or alive!" before fleeing to his horse, a throng of frenzied miners chasing close behind him.

Joaquin lived at a time when racial prejudice was rampant. The *San Joaquin Republican* reported, "If an American meets a Mexican he takes his horse, his arms and bids him leave." And, at the time of Joaquin's reign of terror, a Mexican accused of nothing more than "acting in a suspicious manner" was almost lynched by an hysterical mob. Thus, when the California State Legislature authorized a ruthless bounty hunter by the name of Harry Love to lead a posse to bring back Joaquin dead or alive, there was concern that Love might simply murder the first Mexican he found who vaguely fit Joaquin's uncertain description.

After a little over two weeks on the trail, Love's California Rangers captured a man they suspected of being Joaquin's brother. Whether he actually was the bandit's brother will never be known as he and two others accused of being thieves were killed before they could reach the Quartzburg jail. As one of the posse members explained years later, "It took too much trouble to carry prisoners about with us and when we were sure of a man being a bandit we shot him or hung him."

A few weeks later reports indicated that Joaquin had fled to Southern California and was heading for the safety of Mexico. Love turned south and searched the Coast Range but time was running out. His men had reached the end of their endurance and angrily discovered that their expense allowance of one hundred and fifty dollars a month was woefully inadequate. Love knew his men would not stay with him much longer when, on the morning of July 24, 1853, he and his men came upon an encampment of six to eight Mexican horseman. All but two guards were asleep. Without warning, Love's men descended upon the camp. The Mexicans attempted to escape but the Rangers were too fast for them. One of Love's men, a man who later claimed to have known Joaquin Murrieta years before, suddenly pointed toward the leader and shouted, "This is Joaquin, boys! We've got him at last."

At once the camp was ablaze with gunfire as the Mexicans made a desperate bid for freedom. The man identified as Joaquin jumped onto his horse and, with only a lariat as a bridle, leapt fourteen feet over the edge of a creek into the dry river bed as the posse galloped after him. The rider fell off as his mount slipped and tumbled in the sand but, within moments, he was back on the horse riding for his life. Moments later, a lead ball struck him in the back. Then he was hit again, followed by a shot to the head. The rider fell from his horse. As he tried to stand, he cried out to his pursuers to stop their firing but his pleas were to no avail. Within moments, he was cut down by gunfire.

Upon examining the man they had killed, the posse found that their victim had blue eyes and light brown hair. Joaquin had been described as having black hair and dark eyes. Still the man had a scar on his face and Joaquin was said to bear such a scar. Love ordered that the man's head be severed from his body and the "proof" of their success was placed in a keg of brandy for transportation back to San Francisco. When the man who had identified "Joaquin" was asked years later if it really was the famous bandit they had killed, he said, "One pickled head was as good as another if there was a scar on the face and no one knew the difference."

Back in San Francisco the pickled head was placed on display in a jar where the curious paid a dollar apiece to see it. The *San Francisco Daily Herald* printed a letter sent to them by someone claiming to be Joaquin Murrieta in which the writer assured the editor that, despite stories to the contrary, he was still in possession of his own head. Others who had known him, including James W. Marshall, the discoverer of gold in California, and a woman claiming to be Joaquin's sister agreed that the unfortunate head in the jar was not that of the celebrated bandit. Many years later, a man who introduced himself as Joaquin's nephew told San Francisco historian, Samuel Dickson, that his uncle had wisely retired to a peaceful life in Sonora, Mexico where he became the patriarch of a large family.

Over the years the head in the bottle passed through a number of hands before ending up in Dr. Jordan's Museum of Horrors on San Francisco's Montgomery Street where it is believed to have been destroyed during the earthquake and fire of 1906.

But that was not to be the end of Joaquin Murrieta in San

Francisco. George Barron, once the curator of the de Young Museum, used to tell of an old brick house which once stood on Dolores Street across from the mission. It was here that Joaquin, dressed in clothes befitting a Spanish Don, was said to have attended dances when visiting the city, and, according to tradition, relieved his fellow guests of their jewels and other valuables. Years later, when the house stood ruined and abandoned his ghost was said to be seen at night by those who dared look inside through the weathered window frames. The sound of laughter and the music of Spanish guitars was often heard to echo from within the vacant building while trees near the house were said to shake violently though not even a light breeze could be felt in the air.

One night, to win a wager, a neighborhood saloon keeper ventured inside the mysterious house. As he looked around in the decaying old kitchen, he suddenly heard three ear-splitting rifle shots and turned just in time to see a shadowy gray figure run past him and rush up the stairs without making a sound.

Till the day it was torn down, Spanish women obliged to pass the house at night on their way to church fearfully crossed themselves as they walked by.

# Waiting in the Rain

The rain poured relentlessly, obscuring their vision and making driving hazardous as Sam Kerns and his companion carefully drove down Mission Street returning home from a party late one night. As they approached First Street, Kerns gradually perceived the faint form of a young woman standing alone on the corner as if waiting for someone. Drawing closer, they were surprised to find that she was dressed only in a thin white evening gown and had neither a coat nor umbrella. Yet she seemed oblivious to the weather. Thinking that she might be in trouble, Kerns pulled up to the curb and asked if they might give her a ride home.

"Yes, thank you very much," she answered and the men quickly helped her into the back seat of their coupe. As she was obviously cold and wet, Kerns wrapped a car blanket around her. She volunteered an address near Twin Peaks where she said she lived with her mother but offered no explanation as to how she had become stranded. And, although she answered politely when spoken to, it was clear that her mind was on something else and she remained, otherwise, strangely silent.

As they passed Fifth Street, Kern's companion turned around for a moment to make certain that she was all right. To his horror, the back seat was empty! Thinking she might have fainted, he quickly leaned over the seat only to find the wet and discarded blanket lying on the floor.

Immediately, he told Kerns to pull over and they attempted to sort out an explanation. They had both seen and spoken with the girl and, yet, she had disappeared without a trace. They had not made any stops and, even if they had, as their car had only two doors, it would have been impossible for her to have left the car without their having known it.

There was only one way to discover an answer and the they began searching out the address given by their mysterious passenger.

They soon found the place and, despite the late hour, a pale light shown from within the sadly neglected house. Hesitantly, they knocked on the front door. It was some time before the sounds of footsteps were heard from within. The two men waited expectantly, wondering what they would say. At last the door opened to reveal a frail, elderly woman huddled beneath a shawl. Kerns felt uncomfortable as he started to explain the reason for their visit but the old woman seemed to understand and sympathetically placed her hand over his.

"Yes, I know," she gently interrupted. "You needn't continue. It has happened before. That was my daughter. She was killed in an automobile accident two years ago at the corner of First and Mission. She has often tried to return home."

# The Ghosts of Golden Gate Park

It was not yet dawn and a gentle cloak of darkness still hung over the landscape as cement magnate, Arthur Pigeon, and several lady friends leisurely drove through Golden Gate Park on the morning of January 5, 1908. All seemed peaceful and calm, with only the sound of the motor and the chatter of his companions intruding upon the tranquillity of the park, when, suddenly, one of the ladies let out a scream.

There, looming up before them in the path of his headlights, Pigeon saw an eerie luminous figure in a white robe reaching out its arms as if in an attempt to stop the vehicle. Immediately he reached for the throttle, turned the wheel, sent the automobile swerving around the apparition and continued on at top speed for almost half a mile until he was flagged down by mounted policeman, D. A. Daly.

Hesitantly, Pigeon pulled over to the side of the road and took a moment to collect himself before addressing the patrolman. "We saw a ghost!" he said in a trembling voice.

"Sure you did," said Officer Daly. "I'll bet you've seen lots of spirits tonight — the kind that come out of a bottle."

"No, it's the truth," cried out one of the women, her pale face and terrified eyes lending credence to the story.

Still the officer was suspicious. "Well, why don't you show

me this spook and I'll see to it that he spends a night in jail."

The women became almost hysterical, declaring that nothing on earth would induce them to face the glowing phantom again.

Pigeon was no more eager to volunteer than his guests but, reluctantly, as the ladies quickly alighted from the automobile, he agreed to show Daly where the ghost had appeared.

As Pigeon cautiously drove back, Daly trotted on horseback alongside him, his revolver drawn. They arrived at the spot just as the sun began to rise. Pigeon pointed to a tall cypress tree softly bathed in the morning light and whispered, "That's where it was. Right in front of that tree."

The policeman rode over to the tree, his pistol at the ready, and searched the area. The phantom seemed to have faded away into the morning mists.

Again Daly suggested that, perhaps, the ghost might have been the result of a visit to one of the roadhouses along the beach but Pigeon remained adamant in his story.

"It was a tall, thin figure in white," he maintained, "and it seemed to shine. It had long, fair hair and was barefooted."

"What about its face?" Daly asked.

"His face?" Pigeon answered in surprise. "I was too frightened to get a good look. I just wanted to get away as fast as I could."

The ladies all agreed as to the details of Pigeon's story and Captain Gleeson of Park Station ordered that any ghost matching the description they had given be arrested on sight. None of his men, however, volunteered to bring the phantom in and we can only assume it is still at large, prowling about the park.

If so, it would not be the only ghost to haunt Golden Gate Park for, if you walk along the path between the Lindley and Speedway Meadows at dusk, heading east to where the path ends at Marx Meadow, you might see, as the first Park Superintendent, John McLaren, and others have over the years, a melancholy young woman dressed in purple standing by the main drive, waiting to be offered a ride home, only to vanish as night falls or upon reaching the park entrance.

Stories are also told of a phantom police officer who pulls over drivers in the park and gives them a ticket for speeding – a ticket which never makes its way through the court system – for the startled motorist later learns that tickets issued by the officer in question are never processed due to his having died over a decade earlier. It is further alleged that if this particular officer should start to follow you through the park, you need only drive as far as the nearest park exit where the phantom patrolman always disappears just before crossing the park boundary.

Nestled within the gentle waters of Stowe Lake, lovely Strawberry Hill is haunted at night by the spirit of a young woman said to be searching for her baby. Some say that she was enjoying a pleasant day boating on the lake in the late 1800's when her infant child fell out of the boat, sinking beneath the waters. Panic stricken, the woman dove into the water attempting to save her child but, in the end, both of them perished.

Others tell a darker tale, whispering that in 1920's or the 1930's a woman had become pregnant and, after concealing her condition from her family and giving birth in secret, the distraught mother had abandoned the child on the small island and then drowned herself in the lake.

Whatever the true story may be, numerous visitors to the park have told of seeing the pathetic form of a bedraggled young woman with long dark hair in a white dress, now discolored by the elements, desperately searching Strawberry

Hill and the shores of Stowe Lake.

And then there is the ghostly silver-gray wolf said to haunt the park at night, howling when the moon is full.

Finally, years ago, there was "The Banshee of Golden Gate Park," a fearsome white wraith with large glowing eyes which flew through the night filling the air with its bloodcurdling, screeching cries. This, however, was a specter which can today be seen stuffed and mounted in the park's California Academy of Sciences Museum. For it was only a great white owl, somehow lured thousands of miles from its native habitat north of the Arctic Circle and, sadly, hunted down by a park grounds keeper.

# The Sixteenth Street Terror

An extremely dangerous entity haunted a Mission district apartment on Sixteenth Street during the 1970's. From almost the first night, Joseph Harker, then a twenty-five-year-old political science student at San Francisco State University, felt there was something unusual about the place. The entire atmosphere was oppressive and an air of hostility surrounded him as if in silent anticipation of things to come. His friends had noticed it too.

The silence, however, was not to last. Joseph soon began to hear unexplainable noises and strange muffled voices in the middle of the night. The voices seemed as though engaged in conversation but they were never distinct enough for him to actually understand.

Hoping to find a logical explanation, Joseph asked his next door neighbor if he could possibly be causing the mysterious noises. "No," the neighbor answered but he had been meaning to talk to Joseph as he had also heard them. And even more perplexing, he had heard them in the weeks before Joseph had moved in, at a time when the apartment was completely empty. As there were only two apartments on that floor, they could ferret out no plausible explanation.

A few nights later, at about two in the morning, Joseph

heard a grinding sound coming from his front door. As he walked down the hall to investigate, he was startled to see the heavy glass and wood door bow inward toward him as if someone with enormous strength were pushing against it. His heart pounding, he drew closer and observed that the door was now bending inward three or four inches beyond the door frame. Then, suddenly, the knob turned and the door slowly opened. No one was there. No more than a breath of wind stirred outside and, if someone had been playing a prank, he would have easily seen or heard them fleeing down the two flights of metal staircase which led up to his apartment.

On his tenth night in the apartment, Joseph awoke with a start at about 3:00 AM. "It was as if my dreams were being pushed out of my head," he later recalled. "I opened my eyes and saw a woman walking down the hall past my bedroom. She seemed as if from another era." She had eastern European features, long auburn hair and was dressed in a white shroud-like gown. She appeared to move or float in a trance-like state, seemingly unaware of his presence.

Some nights the disturbing voices and malevolent atmosphere became so frightening that he felt compelled to flee his apartment, spending the rest of the night in an all-night sandwich shop a block away.

Finally on October 10, 1976, Joseph Harker experienced the most terrifying night of his entire life. He was awakened by horrible grinding sounds, threatening voices and nerve-shattering bangs which he described as sounding as if someone were smashing barrels with a sledge hammer. As the noises became louder and louder, Joseph hid huddled under the covers, refusing to open his eyes. At last, however, the noises became so unbearable that he just had to look. He opened his eyes and observed every object in his room to be violently bouncing up and down, leaping several inches up into the air.

Then he felt the presence of the woman he had seen before and sensed from her a feeling of intense hatred. At the same time, he found himself moving toward the bedroom window. "It was as if I were being pushed over to the window," he later explained, "and as I was moving toward it, I realized that something wanted me to jump out that window!" Only by summoning all of his will power was he able to overcome that evil force and escape from the room.

The next morning he scoured the telephone book calling anyone he thought might be able to help from metaphysical bookstores to clergymen and psychiatric institutes. Some were sympathetic. Others merely hung up on him. At length he was referred to the author and I agreed to meet him at his apartment the following evening.

A highly psychic friend came along with me and I suggested that, before hearing the details of the haunting, we first walk through the apartment trying to gather whatever impressions we could by ourselves.

We both felt certain areas, especially the bedroom and a particular spot in the hallway, might be associated with the haunting. I felt a cold, shivering sensation while my friend felt dizzy and almost nauseous while in these parts of the house. Joseph later confirmed that these were precisely the same areas in which he had earlier witnessed ghostly manifestations. I also seemed to see small dark spots in the hallway although it was well lit by two overhead lights. It could well have been just my imagination but Joseph commented that he had, also, quite often seen what he described as "black holes" in that same part of the hallway.

As he began to tell of his experiences, I had the opportunity to observe him closely. Thin and bearded, his face clearly showed the strain he had been under for the last few weeks. From talking with him, I could easily see that he was highly intelligent and not prone to being carried away by his imagination. He had no previous interest in psychic phenomena and had never before believed in the existence of ghosts. In the months to come I would get to know him better and come to trust his honesty implicitly.

At about 10:30 that night, Joseph went to bed while my friend and I camped out in the dining room, hoping to experience the ghostly phenomena ourselves.

Sometime between two and four in the morning we were startled to hear a voice scream from within Joseph's bedroom, "Get out! All of you get the hell out of here!" We both rushed into the bedroom only to find Joseph wide awake and bewildered as to why we had run into his room. He had been awake for about half an hour, unable to sleep as he felt something was about to happen. He had not, however, heard the voice which had caused us to leave our post.

In the weeks which followed the house was visited by a celebrated British psychic who offered his impressions concerning the haunting but, to my knowledge, the mystery was never adequately explained. When last I heard from Joseph, the ghost was as active as ever.

# The Curse of Sutro Heights

We shall never know what loss, what irreparable sadness or cruel turn of fate led her to that most final of all decisions. We shall never know the anguish she felt as she made her way along the gracefully winding paths that night past broad terraces of exotic flowers, trees and shrubs which gently perfumed the night air, past statues which loomed before her, lit eerily by the moon, past the crenelated granite parapet and finally down the steep stone steps to the *"Dolce Far Niente"* balcony below.

We shall never know why she chose this particular place. Perhaps it had once been the scene of a happier time and of a memory held sacred within her heart. Perhaps on warm sunlit days she had come here as a child with her family to lose herself in the magnificent fairy tale gardens which Adolph Sutro had created overlooking the great Pacific. Perhaps she had come here at twilight, a lover protectively holding her in a warm embrace as the sky shone red and orange over the sea and, there, had dared to steal a secret kiss. Perhaps, as she wiped away the tears, she stopped, one last time, to listen to the roar of the surf as it crashed onto the rocks below, gazed wistfully down onto the bright lights of the Cliff House and, one last time, dreamed of joys which might have been.

We shall never know. At that moment, the flame of life which had once glowed so brightly within her flickered and grew smaller and smaller until it seemed to exist no longer and, sobbing, she threw herself over the precipice, down onto the rocks below.

Ever since that night, her spirit has been seen crying out through the night from the *"Dolce Far Niente"* balcony. And ever since, stories have persisted of a sinister unearthly force haunting the Heights, waiting to lure the unwary to their death — a force which may have taken over the thoughts of this now almost forgotten woman at a vulnerable moment or, perchance, pushed her with unseen hands. Just conjecture you say? Perhaps. But, then, how else could we explain the mystery behind a second death at that same very place — the death of Beatrice Lewis?

Beatrice Lewis was a well known ballet dancer, choreographer and dance instructor who drew from the gardens of Sutro Heights the inspiration for what might have been the most successful ballet of her career. One day, while walking amidst the statues which then still graced the park, she came upon the idea of presenting a ballet entitled, *A Night at Sutro Gardens*, in which Sutro's statues would descend from their pedestals after nightfall and dance about the enchanted gardens.

It may seem strange to call the gardens enchanted now but in the early 1900's they seemed enchanted indeed. They were, at one time, considered "the pride of San Francisco." When Adolph Sutro, who had made his fortune from the Comstock mines of Nevada and then increased it through wise investments in San Francisco real estate, first saw the heights, there was nothing more to be found at that spot than a spectacular view amidst sand dunes, rocks and a lupine bush clinging to life here and there. But Adolph Sutro was a man of vision. He had proved that before when he saved the flooded Comstock mines by digging a four mile long drainage tunnel under Virginia City. He had been fought by powerful financial interests bent on stopping him and he had personally faced danger and hardship at every turn as he worked side-by-side with his men, setting off dynamite charges and swinging a pick under sweltering conditions. It was backbreaking work but he prevailed and became known as the "King of the Comstock."

The once middle-class German emigrant later set about to build his home on the heights with the same fearless enthusiasm. Under his supervision, the sand dunes were tamed and covered with rich loam, hundreds of trees were planted and wide drives and secluded paths were cut into the landscape. White-painted cast concrete copies of Greek and Roman statues were placed alongside hundreds of gnomes, elves and animals of all kinds amidst lush lawns, carpets of flowers planted in colorful artistic designs and hedges carefully sculpted into fantastic topiary forms. To quote a guidebook of the time: "the result has surpassed even his expectations. The wilderness of sand has bloomed and blossomed into a scene of fairy-like beauty."

He opened his park to the public in 1885 and, over the years, thousands of visitors, including such luminaries as President Benjamin Harrison, Andrew Carnegie and Oscar Wilde passed through the ornate carpenter gothic gates to enjoy Adolph Sutro's gift to the city.

For years afterward, Sutro Heights drew delighted visitors of all ages and Sutro dreamed of adding a library and museum to house his collection of rare books and curiosities. It would be a place where great scholars would come and work amidst the beauty of his home. But in August of 1898, shortly after having served a term as mayor of San Francisco, Adolph Sutro died and his ashes were interred within the stone parapet below his magnificent mansion.

Despite an attempt on the part of his heirs to maintain the estate as Sutro would have wished, it quickly became too great a financial burden and, over the years, as one after another of the grounds keepers were let go, the gardens and their fanciful edifices slowly fell into decay. In 1920, Sutro's daughter, Dr. Emma Merritt, gave the property to the city of San Francisco with the understanding that after her death it would be "forever held and maintained as a free public resort or park under the name Sutro Heights." In 1939, one year after she passed away, employees of the Works Progress Administration pulled down all but one of the buildings and carted off a number of statues. Over the years, time, weather and vandalism all chipped away at the once proud gardens. Today Sutro Heights is only a forlorn shadow of what it once was.

But Adolph Sutro's gardens were still a place of enchantment when the beautiful blond dancer tried out her new ballet, herself dancing the role of Venus, and found it to be so successful that, a few months later, in March of 1940, she was making plans to present the ballet at the Golden Gate International Exposition on Treasure Island.

She felt the piece needed a little polishing here and there and that it required a stronger ending. So she began spending time wandering about the gardens in the hope of again finding just the right inspiration.

On March 20, she invited a friend to come along with her to the heights but her friend had other plans and Beatrice made the visit on her own. After walking through the gardens, she made her way to the "*Dolce Far Niente*" balcony below the parapet and crawled under a fence to sit on a rock at the very edge of the steep cliff.

Two hundred and fifty feet below, a woman sun-bathing had looked up to the cliff just a little before noon and had seen Beatrice sitting there. A few moments later, the dancer rose and turned as if she were about to leave. The next moment, without apparent cause, she was falling through space, her body twisting and tumbling until it crashed onto the rocks below and rolled onto the Great Highway. A startled motorist screeched to a sudden stop as her broken body fell in front of his car. She died in the ambulance on the way to Park Emergency Hospital.

Suicide was quickly ruled out by the police. She had been enjoying the most successful period of her career and was anxiously looking forward to what promised to be her greatest triumph. Perhaps she had slipped on a patch of ice plant, they theorized. Perhaps. But, then again, perhaps there is some truth to the legend of Sutro Heights. Perhaps there is some unseen malevolent force haunting the Heights. Still waiting — patiently waiting — for its next victim.

# Presidio Ghosts

Long before the Spanish established fortifications at what would become the Presidio, a spirit known to the native inhabitants as El Polin was thought to inhabit the spring which now bears its name. When the Spanish arrived, they shared the secret of its amazing properties with their new neighbors. It was said that if a maiden were to dance by the light of the full moon around the small spring which still flows from amidst the trees standing at the end of MacArthur Avenue and drink of its water, the spirit of El Polin would rise from the spring and smile upon the fortunate maiden. She would then be blessed with many children and eternal bliss.

The virtues of this wonderful spring and its benevolent spirit were so heartily embraced by the Spanish that, in the words of an early historian, "its fame was spread throughout California" and General Mariano Vallejo was to write: "It gave very good water and experience afterward demonstrated that it has excellent and miraculous qualities. In proof of my assertion, I appeal to the families of Miramontes, Martinez, Sanchez, Soto, Briones and others; all of whom several times had twins; and public opinion, not without reason, attributed these salutary effects to the virtues of the water of El Polin, which still exists."

In 1794 the Spanish built a horseshoe-shaped fortress called the Castillo de San Joaquin which was perched high upon a white cliff looming a hundred feet above the entrance to the bay. Its cannon, however, were destined never to be fired in anger, which was just as well, for whenever they were fired in a friendly salute, parts of the fragile adobe walls crumbled into dust. By 1853, when the United States Army decided to level the cliff and construct a new fortress, the old citadel lay in ruins.

Its replacement, Fort Point, was more solidly built. It had stout walls five to twelve feet thick made of brick and granite and, in 1861, its one hundred and twenty-six cannon were manned by two companies of the Third Artillery. Like its predecessor, however, Fort Point never was called upon to defend San Francisco and, by the year 1886, having lost its usefulness, it was abandoned by the army.

The fort was not abandoned, however, by all who had so faithfully served within her walls. In the 1930's stories were told of ghostly soldiers who were heard rushing up the granite steps of the old fort's spiral staircases toward the brick ramparts. Other spirits were said to haunt its dark cave-like chambers and passageways, throwing discarded handspikes and cannon shells about on the stone floor like mischievous children. More recently two guides with the Golden Gate National Recreation Area, while spending the night in the fort, reported seeing a pair of soldiers dressed in Civil War period uniforms standing guard duty up on the seaward wall. Another guide, overseeing a similar overnight stay, awoke to clearly observe a phantom soldier standing only a foot or two from where he had been sleeping.

A ghost of more recent vintage was said to have haunted the former Presidio Playhouse. Known only as George, the ghost is thought to be the troubled spirit of a young enlisted man who, during the time of the Korean War, escaped from the psychiatric ward at Letterman Hospital. After the soldier had been missing for ten days, he was listed as absent without leave.

About six weeks later, in the course of a routine fire inspection, members of the Presidio Fire Department entered the theater which had been boarded up and abandoned for some time. They were greeted by a gruesome sight. Hanging from the end of a rope directly over the center of the stage was the lifeless body of the missing soldier.

When the Playhouse again opened its doors, actors and technicians found strange things happening in the theater. Props, lights and chairs would suddenly vanish and then just as suddenly, reappear somewhere else in the building. On other occasions "weird noises" which always defied explanation were heard issuing from dark recesses of the theater. For over twenty years, until the Playhouse was torn down in 1975, the ghostly phenomena continued and, whenever anything bizarre or unexplainable occurred, someone would throw up his hands in frustration and place the blame on George, the theater ghost.

During the army's tenancy at the Presidio, other ghosts were reported haunting the officers' quarters on Funston Row. A soldier in a Civil War style uniform was seen sitting at the breakfast table one morning in one of the residences. Still another of the Funston Row homes was said to be visited by ghostly children who left their footprints in the dust of the attic whenever a couple without children of their own moved in.

Unspecified ghostly activity has also been rumored to occur within the walls of the old Coast Guard Station at Crissy Field.

By far the most intriguing of the Presidio's haunted landmarks, however, is Building Number 2, which stands at the corner of Funston and Lincoln and once housed the Presidio Army Museum. Originally built in 1864 as the Post Hospital, work began late in 1973 to convert the old Italianate and Greek Revival building into a museum. One of those working on the project was living in the basement at the time when, one day, he felt something clasp him firmly about the shoulders. As no one else was in the room at the time, he quickly decided to find other quarters.

Similar phenomena would be experienced time and again by many who visited or worked in the museum. Some felt a sinister, evil presence at the top of a staircase leading up to the second floor while others fled the building in terror after having seen something frightening or experiencing an unexplainable atmosphere of dread.

No one, however, had as many ghostly experiences in the building as a former curator at the museum whom, for the sake of anonymity, I shall identify only as Ed. His first encounter with the paranormal came early on while working in the basement on a saddle for an exhibit. Upon taking a step or two away from his work, he felt something solid blocking his path, as if he had inadvertently run into someone, although no other living soul was in the room.

Then there was the day a woman left the museum just before closing time. She mentioned how much she had enjoyed the exhibits and was particularly enthusiastic about the man in uniform she had seen walking around upstairs. Ed was puzzled. He felt certain no one else had been upstairs and knew it would be very unlikely that anyone in uniform from the post would be free to visit the museum at that particular hour. But the woman had left before he had a chance to realize just how strange her comment was and, by then, it was too late to ask for details.

He locked the door and proceeded to search upstairs for the mysterious soldier. The floor was entirely deserted but, inexplicably, something made him look downward. There at his feet was a Civil War era cap badge in the form of a number three. To his astonishment, this was something for which he had been searching for some time. As the Presidio had been first garrisoned during the American era by the Third Artillery,

Ed had long wished to find a hat badge displaying the number three to place on a Hardee hat in an exhibit showing the uniform of an early Presidio soldier. Despite his best efforts, however, he had been unable to obtain such a badge. But now, there at his feet, was the very artifact for which he had been looking. No "rational" explanation was ever found for its appearance and it was placed on display where unsuspecting visitors were able to see what might, possibly, be considered to be solid, tangible evidence of the museum's ghost.

In the days which followed, from time to time, out of the corner of his eye, Ed began to see what might have been "the man in uniform" the woman visitor has mentioned. He was a dirty, bearded man in an extremely soiled uniform dating to the Civil War period. Wearing a greatcoat with a tattered cape and large muddy boots, his hand grasping the pommel of his sword and a scowl upon his face, the soldier walked about the museum in a fast and agitated manner.

On another occasion Ed turned a corner upstairs into a hallway near the spot where many had previously felt an evil presence. To his horror, he saw a disembodied face floating in the air. It was the heavily wrinkled face of an old man illuminated by innumerable rays of light which seemed to shoot out into the air in all directions.

But not even this encounter would prepare Ed for the most baffling day of all. One morning, as Ed and another employee were in the process of opening the museum, they were surprised to see a soft drink can darting about the porch as if someone were kicking it, although not a breath of wind was to be felt. A bit later, the coworker called Ed over to where he was working to witness something incredible. A piece of mat board he had just cut had suddenly begun to spin round and round. As the two men stared in amazement, the board continued to spin for a least fifteen minutes.

That night, after Ed had closed up and left the building, a man and woman who had visited the museum earlier remained on the porch talking. A short time later Ed got a call from the post's military police saying that the sensors inside the museum had been tripped triggering the burglar alarm. By the time he got back to the museum, Ed found that the alarm had stopped as mysteriously as it had started. The couple, who had remained on the porch all the while, were extremely excited. "You should have seen it! It was like a light show inside," one of them exclaimed, and began to describe the intense display of lights they had seen shooting through the windows during the incident with the alarm. Ed investigated but, as would always be the case when the alarm would mysteriously sound, no one could be found inside the building.

More than once the sound of phantom footsteps and unexplainable reflections of light have been reported in the old building and, once, a man who had often scoffed at the stories told about the museum decided to spend Halloween by himself inside the building in the hope of putting an end the ghost stories once and for all. He hastily left the museum around midnight. All he would ever say about his experience that evening was, "It got very weird!"

# Chinatown Haunts

Past the Grant Street Dragon Gate and beyond the colorful store fronts, within secluded alleys and behind closed doors, Chinatown holds many hidden secrets.

Beginning in 1882, when the United States Congress passed the first of three laws barring all but a select few affluent members of the Chinese community from bringing their wives and families to their new homes in the States, the unacceptable ratio of women to men combined with a legal prohibition against Chinese men marrying non-Chinese women, resulted in what became known as the "yellow slave trade." Chinese girls and young women were kidnaped or sold by their impoverished families and sent by ship to San Francisco where they were either smuggled on shore or represented to be the wives or daughters of the few Chinese exempted by the law. Once on American soil, they were sold into slavery. Those in their teens or older were forced into prostitution and rarely survived the bestial conditions of their servitude for more than five years, while the youngest were forced into lives of brutal labor and unconscionable punishments as "*Mui Tsai's*" or house servants. Once they reached an appropriate age, however, they, too, were often condemned to lives as prostitutes.

Amidst these nightmarish circumstances arose an unlikely heroine. In 1895 Donaldina Cameron, then twenty-five years of age, came to the Occidental Mission Home for Girls in Chinatown intending to serve there for a year's time as a sewing teacher. She soon, however, found herself completely immersed in the dangerous business of rescuing these unfortunate girls from their masters and fiercely protecting them within the sanctuary of the Mission Home. With the aid of city police who, armed with axes and sledgehammers, under the cover of night, raided Chinatown's cribs and brothels, she quickly became adept at finding slaves who had been hastily secreted beneath floors or within recesses behind false walls. To the slave owners and the Tong lords who ran the slave trade, each girl rescued could mean the loss of as much as a thousand dollars. To these men, Donaldina became known as *"Fahn Quai,"* " the white devil," while, to the girls she rescued, she was *"Lo Mo,"* which meant "old mother."

Cameron remained at the Mission Home for almost four decades, becoming its Superintendent in 1900 and, in 1942, the building which she erected at 920 Sacramento Street after the original Mission Home succumbed to the 1906 earthquake and fire was renamed the Donaldina Cameron House.

The threat of a counterattack by the Tongs always loomed ominously over Mission Home and it was said that beneath the building there were secret tunnels in which the slave girls could be hidden in times of danger. Although it is believed that the entrances to these tunnels were bricked up years ago, staff and visitors to Cameron House have reported hearing footsteps and the sound of someone knocking on the other side of the brick wall as well as the plaintive moans, cries, whispers and screams of women and, from time to time, an anxious voice pleading, "Shhh, be quiet!"

A much more pleasant nineteenth century specter is Big Jim Chin, a tall man who had been a merchant in the 1880's. Those fortunate enough to encounter Big Jim strolling the streets of Chinatown have no reason for fear, however, as he is a benevolent spirit who is said to help families facing periods of financial hardship by leaving them money or food. Every twelve years, when Chinese New Year arrives in the year of the dragon, he has been seen carrying sacks of rice which he deposits on the doorsteps of the needy. He is, perhaps, a bit reticent, however, when it comes to making actual contact with his many admirers for, whenever anyone rushes up to greet him or attempts to follow him, he promptly disappears.

Men playing chess in Portsmouth Square, where the first schoolhouse in San Francisco once stood and where, in 1846, the American flag first proudly waved as Captain J. B. Montgomery claimed the city for the United States, speak of how sometimes their chessboard often inexplicable flips over, throwing the chess pieces up into the air. They believe the mischievous spirits of the white children who once went to school there to be responsible and the ghost of a little blond haired boy has been caught in the act, running away giggling after upturning the board only to then vanish as suddenly as he had appeared.

The Chinese Playground on Sacramento between Stockton and Grant has also been the scene of many an encounter with unseen entities. It is here that an Asian lady dressed entirely in white with long black hair has been observed standing atop a fifteen foot high lamppost only to vanish a few moments later and it is here that a little boy's shoe was said to have filled with blood, completely soaking his sock although, after a thorough examination of his foot, not so much as a scratch could be found on him. It is also here that a little boy was once said to have attempted to swing too high and, as a result, fell from the swing, fatally hitting his head on the concrete. Now, in the middle of the night, a particular swing has been known to swing back and forth, higher and higher, as if someone were trying to see how high he can go. It is here that a small girl who was killed when accidentally hit by a boy on a go-cart is said to haunt the playground. And it is here that, twenty or thirty years ago, a Chinese girl was said to have been raped by a local gang and, as a result, became pregnant. After her baby was born she is believed to have buried it, while still alive, somewhere in the playground only to be killed by those same gang members when, sometime later, she felt compelled to return to the playground and retrieve her child. It is said, at night, her tormented spirit still prowls the playground attempting to find her killers and the phantom cries of a baby can sometimes be heard by those who walk by the playground after dark.

In an alley near the Chinese Playground the wraiths of two Asian women with long black hair, glowing red eyes and black ropes around their necks have been seen. They are believed to be the spirits of women who hung themselves rather than continue living with their abusive husbands.

Theaters are often known to harbor a ghost or two and Chinatown's theaters are no exception. At the Great Star Movie Theater on Jackson Street, a patron remembers well the day when he courteously rose from his seat to allow a woman to more easily enter his row and seat herself beside him. He felt her presence there beside him throughout the entire film and when, upon its conclusion, he again arose to allow her to exit only to find that she had mysteriously vanished.

While checking her hair in a restroom mirror at the Great Star, a woman once reported hearing a female voice behind her asking, "How tall am I? Am I tall enough?" Upon turning around to answer, the woman was surprised to find that she was completely alone. She turned back around to the mirror only to hear, once more, the voice ask,"How tall am I? Am I tall enough?" Unable to discern anyone but herself in the mirror, she, again, turned back around. This time, however, she found standing before her a woman over seven feet tall and fled the restroom in terror.

The ladies' restroom at the Pagoda Palace Movie Theater on Powell Street is thought to be haunted as well ever since the time a woman utilizing the facilities suddenly noticed that two feet had mysteriously appeared in the stall next to hers. She was absolutely certain that both stalls had been unoccupied when she had entered the restroom and was equally certain that no one could have entered the restroom without her hearing the opening or closing of the door. Her musing over the strange situation was dramatically cut short, however, when a hideous cackling sound suddenly filled the air! She, too, fled the restroom in terror.

The building at 1021 Grant Avenue, built in 1925 as the Mandarin Opera House and renamed the Sun Sing in 1949, is haunted by the ghost of a former opera star who hung herself in the rear of the building after being spurned by a producer with whom she had been intimately involved.

Some Chinese parents are reluctant to allow their children to join the Chinatown YMCA at 855 Sacramento Street, long rumored to be haunted by the ghosts of bachelors said to attack unsuspecting young boys. A boy named Jonathon was likewise forbidden to join but, as the apartment in which he lived did not have its own bathroom, he secretly became a member. One evening he and some friends decided to drop by the YMCA to take a shower before returning home. While in the shower, one of Jonathon's friends suddenly screamed upon feeling unseen fingers rush up his thigh. Scratch marks proved the truth of his story. Ever since, others have reported similar occurrences.

Two counselors at the YMCA have told of the time when, while playing basketball in the gymnasium, one of them accidentally hit the ball out into an empty hallway. Before they could settle on who would have to run out into the hallway to retrieve the ball, the ball suddenly came bouncing back into the gymnasium where it abruptly stopped directly in front of their feet.

The YMCA pool is also said to be haunted by the ghost of a boy who sneaked into the building after hours through an open window and drowned in the pool. Some, while swimming alone in the pool, have complained of feeling someone grasp them by the leg, attempting to pull them under the water. Others speak of seeing the apparition of a boy standing by the pool or of times when water will begin to ripple as though someone were swimming and wet footprints can sometimes be found leading away from the pool although no one has used the pool for hours.

The YWCA at 965 Clay Street is haunted as well by a young woman who, like many whose husbands were called away into the armed services during the Second World War, took up residence at the YWCA. Upon learning that her husband had been killed in action, the woman hung herself in the North Tower where, from time to time, her ghostly silhouette has been seen and, in one particular spot, the air can inexplicably become icy cold.

The Ping Yeun Housing Projects on Pacific Avenue are also the scene of ghostly encounters. A headless woman has been observed walking about the projects after having committed suicide by jumping from the roof and decapitating herself on a clothesline on her way down. It is also said that screaming can sometimes be heard from within an elevator shaft in which it is believed someone once fell to his death. The unnerving screams of cat which was hung by a boy in a project hallway are said to be still heard as well in the area in which the ghastly act was performed. And, on one of the project rooftops, a volleyball was once observed to roll back and forth as if being kicked by someone on a day in which not a single breeze could be felt.

Taxi drivers might do well to avoid Spofford Alley, where many decades ago Chinese prostitutes plied their trade. It was only a few years ago, when a women dressed in expensive though old-fashioned clothing hailed a cab and asked the driver to take her to the Fairmont Hotel. Upon arriving at her destination, the driver was startled to find that his passenger had unaccountably vanished.

A long time cook at the Chinatown Restaurant at 744 Washington Street has told of how, in the late 1930's, a small boy had been killed from a fall down the staircase while riding his tricycle. Ever since the ghost of a young boy riding a tricycle has been seen upstairs or heard crying in the area of the staircase.

The cook also told of how, in the 1930's, one of his fellow cooks was allowed to sleep in the restaurant kitchen as he had no other place in which to live. Each morning when the man came into work he would see the other cook brushing his teeth in kitchen sink. One day his coworker died but, still each morning, upon entering the kitchen, he would see the ghost of the deceased cook brushing his teeth in the sink. Finally one day he asked the ghost, "What are you doing here?" The spirit merely smiled in a friendly manner and melted into nothingness never to be seen again, although sounds of the ghost carrying out his normal kitchen duties could still be heard from time to time.

The Chinatown Restaurant is also visited every May and June by a phantom Caucasian diner who always sits in the same booth, always asking for a pot of tea and a menu. When the waiter returns to the booth, however, to take the man's order, the customer, whom no one else in the restaurant ever sees, has vanished.

A janitor at the United Commercial Bank at 855 Sacramento Street, in which the Chinatown Telephone Exchange once did business, has told of how, once everyone else has left the premises, as he draws near the back of the building, he can often hear the voices of children, the sound of a ball bouncing up and down and the unmistakable sounds of people playing mah-jongg.

Two final Chinatown hauntings date to times far back in the community's past. The ghost of a little girl with blond hair, wearing a pretty dress from a bygone era, who is believed to have died from a childhood illness, can sometimes be seen walking up and down the same block on Jackson Street with her mother; while at St. Louis Alley strange balls of light have been seen at night flitting about the rooftops and the terrible sight of a man on fire has been observed jumping from a rooftop, across the alley, to the rooftop on the other side in an eternal attempt to escape the flames of the 1906 fire.

# Hoaxes, Humbugs and Other Spurious Spooks

Of course not all ghosts are of supernatural origin. Some result from the misinterpretation of an unusual but none the less natural occurrence while others are due merely to an overactive imagination. Some, however, stem from a deliberate hoax.

In 1913 four men, Paul H. Devine, a private detective; W. P. Neeson, a steamshipman; Lloyd McLoughlin, a café owner and Joseph McLoughlin, a real estate salesman, sat talking around a table at Haggerty's Café at the corner of Waller and Stanyan Streets over a few drinks. They declared that they needed a few drinks after what they had seen. Not far away, around midnight the night before, they claimed to have seen ghosts with horrible glowing faces in the windows of the old, deserted Quigley House in Golden Gate Park and to have heard terrible, unearthly shrieks piercing the evening air.

Their deliberately loud conversation was overheard and soon it seemed as if the whole town was talking about the haunted house in Golden Gate Park. A few nights later, around two hundred fearless souls gathered outside the Quigley House while Paul Devine and Joe McLaughlin, already hidden inside, gave the crowd the scare of their lives by floating handkerchiefs, illuminated from behind by lit cigarettes, in front of the windows, rolling a tin can filled rocks and bolts across the floor and filling the air with bloodcurdling cries.

For six weeks the "ghosts" continued to mesmerize the crowd which, at its outrageous peak, grew to eight hundred. Meanwhile, spiritualists attempted to contact the visitors from great beyond. Even skeptics stared in amazement. Many clergymen came to watch while others warned their flocks to steer well clear of this proof of the devil's handiwork. No one, however, dared to actually venture inside. Lieutenant Bill Dinan of the park police knew the truth about the "ghosts" but he merely smiled and let them have their fun.

It all came to an abrupt end when someone decided to exorcize the spirits by dousing the house with kerosene and lighting a match and the Quigley House burned to the ground.

Almost as great an uproar occurred eleven years later when, on October 1, 1924, the *San Francisco Chronicle* reported: "The City Hall is haunted! A ghost, spook or eerie presence of some sort has created all sorts of excitement in the chambers of the Board of Public Works. Today clairvoyants, Ouija board experts and authorities on spookcraft are invited to attend a seance at noon, sharp."

It had all started about six months before when, one day just a little after noon, John B. Gartland, the attorney for the Board of Public Works, heard five distinct raps on his office wall. Then, a moment later, he heard three more.

Gartland was surprised but did not think much about it until the rapping was repeated at about the same time the next day and then every day thereafter. Not knowing what to do, after months of this he called Louis Tyrrel, the office messenger, in for a listen.

After the clock struck twelve, the two anxiously waited for ten minutes in silent anticipation. Then five raps were heard on the office wall.

"What's that?" Tyrrel asked.

His question was answered by three more mysterious raps.

"My gosh," the messenger gasped. "That's spooks!"

When Timothy Reardon of the Board of Public Works heard about the rapping, he decided something had to be done immediately. "The City Hall," he stated "is no place for ghosts. We've had goats up here before but I draw the line at ghosts."

The next day a crowd of curious observers waited in Gartland's office for the ghosts to present themselves and, right on cue, a little after noon, the rapping began followed by a momentary silence. Then there were three more raps.

"Well, what is it?" Reardon asked the City Architect, John Reid, Jr.

"Search me," the bewildered architect replied and suggested that, perhaps, there was some sort of "natural aerial" somewhere in the building, somehow attracting "certain sound waves every day at a certain time."

The noon-time performance was repeated the next two afternoons and again at midnight on Friday, October 3, for the throngs who were now showing up at all hours. The following day, however, fifty witnesses, including a well-known evangelist and a delegation from the California Psychical Research Society, were all kept waiting an extra fifteen minutes when the ghost failed to make his normal 12:10 "appearance" and delayed his ghostly knocking until 12:25.

Finally, on October 6, the mystery was laid to rest. Two janitors, Sid Hester and an M. Ryan admitted to having produced the spiritual rapping by striking a radiator with a broom. Ryan had accidentally discovered how the sound carried to Gartland's office and, encouraged by his friend Hester, began the rapping as a joke. Their secret might never have been discovered but the janitors decided to end the affair when they started having to put in too many off-duty hours fulfilling their ghostly duties. In the words of a reporter for the *Examiner*, "too many psychical investigators, metaphysicians, faith healers, spirits and spiritualists and others of like and unlike ilk were sticking around the City Hall all hours preventing the janitors from completing their work and retiring to deserved rest."

In the mid-1940's rumors circulated that the neglected old four-story house at 2221 Washington Street was haunted. Through the windows weird flickering lights could be seen moving about throughout the otherwise dark twenty room mansion. But the truth was that Ellinor Davidson, who lived there alone, preferred the past to the present. She had never allowed electricity to be installed in her home and the flickering glow of candles had provided her only source of illumination.

In July of 1961 the house detective at the Palace Hotel was sent out to lay a ghost that had been seen floating outside an upper story window one night. Upon investigation the phantom turned out to be only a flannel nightgown. A guest from Chicago had done her laundry in the bathroom sink and had hung it out in an open window to dry.

Persistent tales of the ruins of Sutro Baths being haunted also date to 1961 when a little man with a pale face and stark white hair mysterious appeared on several occasions before a night security guard patrolling the locked building. Called the "Giggling Ghost" due to the man's habit of laughing in a disconcerting manner at the startled guard, this phantom, also known for his eerie whistling, was almost certainly of the flesh and blood variety. It had left behind muddy footprints and a trip wire was later discovered connected to tape recorder which, when activated, produced ghostly noises.

Perhaps the house most undeserving of a ghostly reputation was the Alexander Russell home on the Great Highway between Ulloa and Vicente Streets. Originally built in 1857 from the wreckage of a ship which had been swept ashore nearby, the place twice served as a tavern before finally being boarded up and abandoned. Years later it was tastefully refurbished by a wealthy gentleman for use as his own home. Following his occupancy in 1901, it again became a popular roadhouse.

Sometime later the Russells bought the house and enclosed it within a fourteen-foot high fence. Almost immediately people began to speculate as to the reason for the fence. The fact that Mrs. Russell was a student of Eastern religion and philosophy and had filled the old house with oriental art and exotic furnishings added fuel to the fire. A weird cult demanding strange and terrible rituals was practiced within by disciples who called Mrs. Russell "Mother," unkind tongues wagged.

It was rumored that skeletons wrapped in winding sheets flew through the cypress trees while ghostly parrots dove down upon anyone so foolish as to come near the house at night. A frightened doctor claimed to have thrown a rock at the spirit of a Tibetan lama and watched in horror as it passed right through his target. And a local baker was allegedly assaulted by a ghost in the vestibule while attempting a late night delivery.

But it was all "bunk" according to writer Ed O'Day who was a friend of the Russells and had spent enough time in the house to know the truth. "That high fence," he said, "was built to keep out but one intruder, the west wind, which was fatal to the plants and flowers. The Russells were the kindest people imaginable. The only cult they ever practiced was that of Christian charity."

In 1917 Mrs. Russell died and her widowed husband sold the house.

A little over a year later, after reopening as Tait's-at-the-Beach, the old house became one of the most successful restaurants in the city. In 1931, however, it fell prey to the Great Depression. Nine years later the house burst into flames and one more colorful relic of San Francisco's past crumbled into ashes.

# The Haunted City

Almost every neighborhood in the city, it would seem, has its haunted house. There was the three-story brick structure which once stood on Telegraph Hill at the corner of Chestnut and Grant. Owned by a retired sea captain by the name of Hane, the house had an evil reputation and mothers cautioned their children against walking on his side of the street when passing nearby. Terrible, shrill screaming could be heard issuing from the upper story at night and an ominous rumbling sound often issued from the parlor. Some even claimed that the entire house swayed and creaked at times like a ship being pitched about in a stormy sea.

Following the Captain's death, two men decided to have a look for themselves and broke into the house. They were searching through a third floor room when a door handle slowly began to turn and the door opened by itself. In the open doorway round lights floated back and forth from the ceiling to the floor only to suddenly vanish and to be replaced by the horrifying form of a man with a wolf's head. The creature watched them for a moment with glaring eyes, barked out as if in warning and then evaporated into the darkness. Within two weeks, one of the intruders was dead.

Similar phenomena was attributed to an abandoned and unfinished house which stood tenantless for seventeen years in the late 1800's at 924 Post Street. The wailing cries of what was believed to be an old man echoed at night through the two and a half story house while the glowing and transparent figure of a gray-haired woman was said to be seen through the broken glass of its windows. One night, just a little after midnight, a disturbance was heard, so loud and violent that the neighbors felt certain the entire house had collapsed. Upon investigation the next morning, however, not a single trace of damage could be found.

And then there was the Mountain Spring House, a roadhouse built by the side of a creek on the old Corbett toll road near Eighteenth Street. Built before the advent of the automobile and popular for a while with local hoodlum gangs, it was frequently the scene of murders and other acts of violence and, as the years passed, it gained a reputation for being haunted. Those who poked around the old place during its last days claimed that the grounds were chillingly cold even on the hottest days of the year. Invisible spirits could be felt to sweep by as a low ghostly voice whispered, "This is the place." Sometimes a soft, dangerously alluring whistling could be heard wafting through the night air and often the ghost of a deer which had been tortured to death and whose antlers had been nailed to the barroom wall was seen to fly in terror through a window.

The Whittier Mansion at 2090 Jackson Street, which, in its time, has served both as the German Consulate for the Third Reich and as the home of the California Historical Society, may hold a dark secret deep within its cellar. Some say it is William Franklin Whittier, who built the red sandstone residence in 1896 and lived there until his death in 1917, having reached the age of 85, whose indistinct form has often been seen lurking down in the basement casting an icy cold chill upon all who encounter him. A former docent at the house, however, begs to differ, having stated, "My theory is that the ghost is his ne'er-do-well son, Billy. The presence is often felt in the basement near the servant quarters and Billy lived for wine, women, and song."

The tall, stately Victorian house at 273 Page Street which seems to have served as everything from a private residence to law offices and a Zen-Buddhist hostel also has a reputation for being haunted. Chandeliers have been observed to swing about without reason while locked doors have been said to open and close by themselves. Ghostly banging has been heard resonating through the house at night and flashing balls of light and ghostly forms have been seen moving through its elegant rooms.

In another part of town, in November of 1959, five young women sharing an apartment on the third floor of a building on Broadway dating back to before the earthquake and fire of 1906 began to wonder about strange things happening in their home. At first it was just the unshakable feeling that someone else was there in the apartment, sometimes following them but always watching.

Then, after a while, they began to hear things. First there was the deep sighing. "It was a weary sigh, as if someone were tired of it all," Barbara Brockway, one of the women living there was later to state. And then there were the footsteps. "Old houses creak," she continued, "but this sound was rhythmical, unmistakably someone walking." One Sunday morning the women not only heard the footsteps but the door slam as well.

Equally disconcerting was the hallway light. "It kept being turned on in the early morning hours," Miss Brockway remembered. Each woman promised to make certain it was off before she went to bed but each morning they would find the light to have been switched back on.

Finally, in mid-January of 1960, at two o'clock in the morning, Brockway actually saw the ghost standing in her bedroom. For some reason she had suddenly awakened from her sleep. "I looked across the room," she recalled, "and there she stood by the dresser. An old woman, slight, with a shawl about her shoulders. Her dress was ankle length and she was standing there looking at me. Her clothing appeared to be of the style worn at the turn of the century. I could not make out her face, except that it was old. She moved and then I saw right through her. She took three steps toward me and then vanished."

When a friend mentioned to two men who had previously lived in the house that it might be haunted, one of them replied casually, "Sure, it's a little old lady."

The final surprise was to come the day a delivery man appeared on the porch with a television. When one of the young women explained that there must be some mistake as none of them had bought a television, the man replied, "I've got orders to deliver this to the little old lady who lives in the back of this place."

In 1963 three young men, Jim Barnes, Charles Letbetter and Ed Sprenger reported poltergeist activity in an old wood-frame house located in the Glen Park district. Not long after moving in, they began to hear footsteps in the attic. Upon investigation they were relieved but mystified to find that no one was there. Next Barnes heard a scratching sound on the wall of the sleeping porch although not a mark was to be found.

One night Barnes was awakened by the sound of his television, which, quite inexplicably, was on, and, even more strangely, was lying on the floor by the side of his bed. He knew the television had been in the living room when he had gone to bed that night but he was too tired to try to find an explanation and, instead, turned it off and went back to sleep. When he awoke the next morning the television was back on again.

The most perplexing mystery of all came when the men returned home from work one day to find that the electricity had been turned off. Sprenger set out for the basement to check the fuse box but found that the key to the basement door, which had always worked before, was now completely ineffectual. They had not been given a key to the padlock on a second basement door and they were unable to open any of the basement windows. Finally, after removing the padlocked door from its hinges, they found that all of the fuses were just fine. The old-fashioned main breaker switch, however, had been thrown into the open position. When Sprenger reset the switch to the "on" position, he saw the connection was far too tight for the switch to have fallen into the "off" position on its own. And, as the basement had been securely locked, no flesh and blood intruder could have entered and thrown the switch!

For over four months the three men heard eerie noises which defied all attempts at explanation and they endured the nuisance of lights going on and off by themselves, a radio which turned on of its own accord and doors which, when locked, would later be found unlocked and, when unlocked, would later be found to be locked.

One day, as Barnes was combing his hair in a mirror in the bathroom, the mirror shattered before his eyes. On another occasion, while talking together outside, Barnes and Sprenger saw what looked like a flash of light shoot through their living room. That night they decided to sleep elsewhere.

Of course it is not only private residences that harbor ghosts. Security guards at the historic Flood Building at Fifth and Market, erected in 1904 on the previous site of the Baldwin

Hotel and Theater and where, during the 1920's, Dashiel Hammett worked for the Pinkerton Detective Agency, have reported hearing a sound similar to that of boxes being struck hard followed by the chilling screams of men, woman and children on the ninth floor. And a woman wearing a nightgown engulfed in flames has been seen frantically running down the hallway. Perhaps these are ghostly echos of the those who died when, in 1898, "Lucky" Baldwin's luck temporarily deserted him and his building burned to the ground.

Other ghosts seem to date to the present building. Max Canton, head of security for the building, has reported, "I feel like something's watching me. I hear 1930's music and, though I wear a blazer and work up quite a sweat walking long halls and climbing stairs, I get a cold chill on the stairwell between the third and fourth floors."

In 1933 Hewlett Tarr, a young box office employee at the Curran Theatre was horrified to, one day, see a revolver thrust at him through the bars of the ticket window. His assailant, a small time hoodlum by the name of Eddie Anderson had intended to demand two tickets to the musical, *Show Boat*, in the hopes of impressing his girlfriend. His plans went terribly awry, however, when his gun was caught within the ticket window grill and accidently fired. Tarr, who had been engaged to be married that Thanksgiving, fell dead onto the floor.

After two weeks on the run, Anderson was caught, convicted of Tarr's murder and met his end on the gallows at San Quentin Prison.

Ever since, from time to time, playgoers at the Curran have reported seeing the reflection of the handsome but ill-stared Hewlett Tarr in the large mirror across from the theater's entrance.

A ghostly woman is said to have been seen in the warehouse

of the San Francisco Orchard Hardware. The unmistakable sound of someone wearing high heels has been reported as well, along with both screaming and laughing. She is said to blow in men's ears and to gain the attention of women sporting long hair with gentle tugs on their tresses. One employee tells of the time that the power went out just after he had just finished shrink wrapping a pallet. When the power was restored a few seconds later, he was startled to discover that the pallet had been completely unwrapped!

Fans of old-time baseball might wish to visit the Safeway at 2300 Sixteenth Street which was built on the former site of the Seals Stadium erected in 1931 for the Seals and the Missions teams of the Pacific Coast League and where the Giants later played for two seasons. Grocery shoppers have often told of seeing phantom baseball players strolling about the produce section and items there have been said to break of their own accord.

Meanwhile, at the 730 Taraval Safeway, the ghostly form of a boy, seven to ten years of age, is said to have been observed haunting the hallway leading to the storage room.

A mansion built by the silver magnate, Richard Chambers, at 2220 Sacramento Street is said to be haunted by his niece, Claudia, who died there under suspicious circumstances. While a newspaper ascribed her death to a "farm implement accident," less trusting souls claimed she was stabbed to death, while others asserted that Claudia was cut in half! Whatever the truth of her death may be, something seems to have caused her and others to remain in the house. When, some years ago, the Chambers house was combined with an adjoining house into a hotel known as The Mansions, numerous stories were told by guests of objects moving about of their own accord and blankets being pulled off their beds at night. Unaccountable noises emanated from unoccupied rooms and empty hallways and apparitions were observed, one of which was said to have been captured in a photograph prominently displayed on a hotel wall.

Although The Mansions was eventually sold and the two houses are now in private hands, there are still a number of San Francisco hostelries in which one might reserve a haunted room.

Originally built in 1902 as the home of railroad titan, Milton Schmidt, and converted into a hotel two years later, the Hotel Majestic, which boasts the title of San Francisco's "the oldest continually operated hotel," also boasts a haunted fourth floor where, late at night the resident ghost walks the corridor, rattling a set of keys against the hallway walls. Unseen hands have been known to fill the bathtub in one room with water and the bed in another room once shook so violently in the middle of the night that a guest erroneously thought San Francisco was experiencing yet another earthquake!

The Queen Anne Hotel at 1590 Sutter Street is believed to be haunted by Mary Lake for whom the Victorian building was built in 1889 by the "Silver King," Senator James Graham Fair, and which opened the following year as Miss Mary Lake's School For Young Ladies.

Although guests have reported feeling her friendly spirit throughout the hotel, it is on the fourth floor and particularly in Room 410, where she once had her office, that her vapor-like form has been most often seen and manifestations of her presence experienced. It is said that she has unpacked guest's luggage for them, replaced fallen pillows onto their bed and, on cold nights, lovingly covered them with extra blankets.

The San Remo Hotel, erected at 2237 Mason Street by Bank of America founder, A.P. Giannini, immediately following the 1906 earthquake and originally christened, The New California Hotel, is said two have two resident ghosts. One spirit, thought to be a former "madam," is said not only to haunt room 33 but to repeatedly knock on the doors of nearby rooms until a guest opens the door only to find that there is no one in the hallway. And then there are the sightings of a little girl wandering the hallway in an eternally vain attempt to enter room 42.

The St. Francis Suite in the famous St. Francis Hotel is said to be haunted by an elegantly dressed lady in a white gown thought to be the spirit of Edith Pope who, with her philanthropist husband, George, resided in that very suite during the 1930's and the 1940's.

At the Sir Francis Drake Hotel an unidentified woman dressed in the style of the 1950's is said to haunt room 1522.

Playwright Lillian Hellman is thought to be one of the many ghosts said to haunt room 207 of the Hotel Union Square, the scene of her affair with Dashiell Hammett. Hellman is blamed for the bathroom door continually opening by itself and for objects flying about of their own accord. Other spirits take the form of inebriates dozing in the hotel hallways, spirits which vanish as hotel guests draw nearer.

Accommodations of a far less enjoyable kind were, from 1859 to 1963, provided on the island of Alcatraz for prisoners, first of the United States military, and, after 1934, of the Federal Bureau of Prisons. Centuries before, the native inhabitants had shunned the island as a repository of evil spirits and its years as a penal facility infamous for unspeakably harsh and cruel conditions only increased the malevolent atmosphere which, to this very day, still permeates the very walls of its crumbling buildings.

Over the years since Alcatraz was opened to the public as a part of the Golden Gate National Recreation Area, park rangers have reported a plethora of ghostly phenomena including the unmistakable sound of metal cell doors clanking shut, horrifying screams and the unshakable feeling that one is being watched.

Although almost all of the island seems to be haunted, Cell Block D is worthy of special note. It was here that incorrigibles were stripped naked and consigned to an excruciatingly cold, windowless cell with only one light which was often turned off at the whim of a guard. And it was here, on Cell Block D, that a spirit with glowing eyes and wearing late nineteenth century clothing was said to prowl the premises. On one occasion a convict confined to "the hole" began to scream that he was being attacked by something with glowing eyes. The guards ignored his anguished cries for help which continued on throughout much of the night. By the next morning the cell was eerily quiet. Upon opening his cell, the prisoner was found to be dead, a look of terror frozen upon his face and the clear marks of strangulation evident about his throat.

Among the many other ghostly phenomena encountered from time to time on Alcatraz have been the temporary reappearance of a long ago demolished lighthouse, a whistling sound attributed to Robert Stroud, the "Birdman of Alcatraz," and the strains of banjo music emanating from within the cell once home to Al Capone who had been a member of a four-man prison band and had spent much of his time playing the banjo in his prison cell.

On a much lighter note, in 1949, a rather comely ghost was reported to haunt a Montgomery Street apartment in a building dating back to the Gold Rush and described as being famous both as the home of numerous artists, poets and writers and as the scene of wild parties, murders and suicides. A famous artist who lived there had been given a key to the apartment next door and had been asked by his neighbor to take a look around the apartment whenever he was out of town to make certain that everything was alright.

On one such occasion he entered the neighbor's apartment at two or three in the morning and took the opportunity to read a little from his friend's library. By the time he had finished reading he was tired and decided to spend the night there. After locking the door and connecting the safety chain, he headed for the bedroom.

He had only retired for a few minutes and had not, yet, drifted off to sleep when he heard the distinctive sound of a woman in high heels walking toward him. He looked up to see a tall, young woman with dark brown hair flowing down to her shoulders.

Without saying a word, the woman walked over to him, sat down on top of him and took hold of one of his hands. Frightened, he jumped up out of bed and, in that moment, the woman vanished. As the artist rushed back to the safety of his own apartment, he was stunned to discover that the door was still locked and chained.

He had decided not to mention his experience to anyone but changed his mind when another of his neighbor's friends, after having spent a night in the place, emerged from the apartment the next day in a highly agitated state.

"That place is haunted!" the friend exclaimed. Exactly the same thing had happened to him.

A ghost with a definite sense of style was said to haunt the Café Charles, the charming restaurant which graced 865 O'Farrell Street in the 1960's. This ghost, described by a woman who had seen him often, was "a person of quality. He wears a well-tailored suit and is accompanied by a white dog on a leash — a thorough gentleman."

A thorough gentleman he may well have been but he was not above playful antics now and again. He was once accused of stealing a full bottle of wine and, on more than one occasion, startled women in the restaurant by speaking a few carefully chosen words or merely issuing forth a suggestive "Psst!" To other gentlemen he made his presence known by flushing the toilet in the men's room.

"He's no fool; this ghost of mine," proprietor Robert Charles once stated with a smile. "He prefers the ladies but does not permit himself to get involved; the true mark of the sophisticate. A softly uttered word, a pat in the right place, perhaps an appreciative pinch and he is gone. He doesn't linger."

While Café Charles is now only a memory, a present day haunted nightspot is the Empire Plush Room at the Hotel York. Originally a Roaring Twenties speakeasy, its then-hidden entrance revealed only after navigating an elaborate system of tunnels, the Plush room offered the cream of San Francisco's elite both forbidden libations and top-rate entertainment. One night Lester, the house pianist, fell over dead in the midst of a performance. The urge which performers feel to entertain, however, never dies and the staff at Plush Room still feel his presence, occasionally encountering a shadow-like phantom and hearing the strains of an otherwise unexplainable tune waft from the piano.

As San Francisco grew in population over the years and the availability of new building sites became scarcer and scarcer, a series of desperate decisions issued from City Hall. There was no longer room for the dead in San Francisco. In 1901 an ordinance was passed "prohibiting the burial of the dead within the City and County of San Francisco." Too much valuable land had been taken up by cemeteries. In 1910 cremation was also banned. By the early 1930's it became clear that even those buried before the turn of the century had to go as well and, one by one, the residents of San Francisco's cemeteries, with the exception of the Mission Dolores Cemetery, the National Cemetery in the Presidio and the National Pet Cemetery, were exhumed and sent off to the newly created "City of the Dead," Colma; their once lovingly erected tombstones consigned to use in retaining walls and as stepping stones.

The process of removing the dead took years and not all of the dearly departed were always found, leaving some remaining to this day beneath the foundations of present day residences and businesses.

The idea of "relocating" San Francisco's dead, however, had even earlier origins. In 1860 the residents of the Hebrew Cemetery, which had been situated in Pacific Heights at Broadway and Vallejo, between Gough and Franklin Streets, were moved to the Gibbath Olum Cemetery, a new Jewish cemetery located in the Mission district at Church and Dolores, between 19th and 20th Streets, before it, too, was closed in 1888 and, in the 1930's its residents were moved, some for the second time, to the Hills of Eternity Cemetery in Colma.

Perhaps, however, interfering with so many soul's final resting places has resulted in more than a few unintended consequences. A young man identified only as John lived, some years ago, in a house located on the site of the former Hebrew Cemetery, a house in which eerie things were known to happen, things so frightening that a priest was finally called in by his family to exorcize whatever might be haunting their home. That night, while the entire family was gathered around the dinner table, the lights began to flicker on and off, followed by every door in the house slamming shut!

Just before John's family finally moved away from the house, one of the children decided to try to capture evidence of the ghost on a tape recorder. "He went downstairs with the recorder and, before he could even turn it on, an evil roar coming out of nowhere brought him upstairs immediately in a panic. He couldn't speak for at least an hour and a half," John's girlfriend, Collete, was later to recall.

On another occasion, Collete and John were to find themselves sitting on a bench in Dolores Park, the former site of the Gibbath Olum Cemetery, when they both felt an ominous presence and distinctly heard the inexplicable sound of clapping behind them. As it was around four in the afternoon, John said, "Let's get out of here before it gets dark!" No sooner had he spoken, however, than the park suddenly became shrouded in darkness. As they hurriedly fled the park, the sound of someone laughing echoed close behind them. "There were only two people in the park mind you: me and my boyfriend," Collete later affirmed

During the nine and a half years it took to relocate most of the bodies from San Francisco's cemeteries, the Richmond district, which had been composed almost entirely of cemeteries, presented many a disturbing sight. Students at the University of San Francisco, built upon what had been the Masonic Cemetery, were known to park their cars in recently vacated mausoleums and, in 1939, the *San Francisco Chronicle* reported tales of thieves breaking into cemetery vaults in order to pilfer silver coffin handles and whatever valuables may have been interred with the dead.

"Here, during the cemetery's abandoned years," the

Chronicle luridly lamented, "tramps piled up their pots and pans; set up their cooking utensils for a macabre type of housekeeping. Some even say that these dank vaults were hideouts for bootleggers, during the prohibition years.

"Other ghouls have wreaked havoc. Bronze and iron-grilled doors of other ornate marble and granite above-ground vaults have been pried open. Inside all is shambles. Flower urns have been ripped from wall braces, coffins hacked open, bones strewn about."

Today, all that remains of the once vast Richmond district necropolis is the Columbarium at One Loraine Court set back behind Geary Boulevard near Stanyan Street. Built in 1897 as the visual focal point for the Odd Fellows Cemetery, the magnificent three story, copper-domed neoclassical repository of cremated remains gradually fell into a state of severe decay after being abandoned in 1934.

When I first visited the Columbarium in the late 1960's it seemed a grotesquely surreal vision from a Victorian "penny dreadful." Raccoons had claimed dominion over alcoves holding brass, silver and marble urns and water slowly oozed down from the leaking roof, both cracking and discoloring the plaster ornamentation and providing sustenance to the fungus which clung like tattered velvet drapery over its once proud walls. With each tentative step I took into the inner sanctum, pigeons and doves flew from the eaves and niches as if sent by unseen masters to dissuade me from venturing any further into their previously silent domain. Little wonder that I felt a disquieting tension, as if someone not of this world were watching me closely.

In 1979 the Columbarium was purchased by the Neptune Society which immediately set about restoring the Columbarium and its surrounding grounds to their former glory. The restoration, however, has done nothing to quell the uneasy feeling that the Columbarium may house more than just the physical remains of the over thirty thousand souls interred within its walls.

On one occasion a visitor was startled to suddenly feel a hand upon her back. Upon turning around she was shocked to find that no one was there – no one she could see that is. But her unseen companion had left a calling card of sorts, an otherwise unexplainable white handprint on the back of her blouse!

# Together

Her hands trembled as she pulled back the curtain and gazed down upon the street below. A gentle rain had just subsided, leaving everything transformed, appearing fresh and new.

"How many things have changed," she thought as she journeyed back to that day so long ago when she had first arrived in San Francisco as a bride.

That was back in 1885 when she married the man she had loved for so many years and, although she was then in her thirties, she had felt eighteen again as he drew her up into his arms and carried her across the threshold of the bridal suite of the Palace Hotel.

He had carefully lowered her to her feet and, holding her with a touch that was a kiss, said, "I'll be back in just a few minutes."

"But why?" she asked.

"Roses. You must have roses."

"Oh, it's not necessary," she responded.

"No, you must always have roses," he whispered as he

cradled her face in his hands and gently kissed her one more time.

While she busied herself with the unpacking and fantasized about the life they were about to begin, he walked from the hotel to a nearby flower stand where he purchased a large bouquet of red roses. Red roses were her favorite.

As he crossed Kearney Street on the way back to the hotel, someone screamed, "Watch out!" But it was too late. A runaway team of horses sped around the corner and, only a moment later, his lifeless body lay there on the street framed within the roses which had fallen from his hand.

Although she gradually seemed to recover from her grief in the weeks which followed, she steadfastly refused to move from the bridal suite. Weeks turned into months and months into years but she continued to live there in those rooms for the next twenty years.

"Wouldn't it be better if you moved?" her friends would gently ask.

"Oh, no," she would always reply. "I could never do that. My husband is here and, if I were to leave, he would have no place to go."

And, although she seemed perfectly rational and normal in every other respect, she always remained faithful to "the presence" with whom she shared her rooms.

That afternoon, as she gazed down onto the street, she suddenly felt a little tired and lay down for a nap, never again to awaken. Perhaps, as she fell asleep, she saw him more clearly than she had seen him before. Perhaps he reached out and gently placed his hand into hers and smiled for those who found her said she had a look of joy and contentment. And though she would be missed by her friends, she would not have wanted them to mourn her passing. She had joined her husband and now, at last, they were free to leave — together.

www.ingramcontent.com/pod-product-compliance
Lightning Source LLC
Chambersburg PA
CBHW061644040426
42446CB00010B/1574